# Shattering Low Expectations

## A Guide for Educators and Parents of American-black Students

by

Ed J. Harris

authorHOUSE™

1663 LIBERTY DRIVE, SUITE 200
BLOOMINGTON, INDIANA 47403
(800) 839-8640
WWW.AUTHORHOUSE.COM

*First published by AuthorHouse 12/06/05*

*ISBN: 1-4208-8434-4 (sc)*

*Printed in the United States of America*
*Bloomington, Indiana*

*This book is printed on acid-free paper.*

*Cover design by Laurie Mueller-Bevirt of Good Cause Communications.*
*Photography by Don Bevirt.*

Another publication by EnTeam: *Win Together in
Education* by Theodore A. Wohlfarth, 2005

**EnTeam Vision Statement**
People can make a more peaceful and productive world by learning to win
together and measuring skill in solving problems collaboratively.

**The EnTeam Mission Statement**
Increase cooperation and raise academic achievement by providing activities that challenge
students, teachers, and communities to win together and measure collaboration.

EnTeam is a 501(c)(3) non-profit organization that offers programs connecting
education with community service, professional development for teachers,
workshops for families, and school transformation services. The people who
provide the services of EnTeam are a network of professionals and volunteers with
experience in varied fields: education, social work, process engineering, school
administration, organizational development, human resources, and research.

The word EnTeam is coined by combining the prefix "en" (meaning to bring
into) plus "team" (a group organized to work together to achieve a goal).
Joy → enjoy. Courage → encourage. Team → enteam.

The word "EnTeam" means organizing diverse peoples into a
united effort to solve problems through collaboration.
Enteam is a registered trademark.

Phone: 636-227-8989          Email: enteam@enteam.org          Web site: www.enteam.org

# Acknowledgements

Thanks to Chrissy, wife extraordinaire, for her understanding and patience during my many hours of writing.

I extend a hearty thank you to the early readers of the manuscript who put in hours of reading and conversation about the topics. Thanks to Sharon Greene, retired teacher and grant writer for EnTeam; Charlotte Prunty, the active parent of three children in the Rockwood School District in the suburbs of St. Louis, Missouri; Flossie Henderson, project director, GEAR UP, St. Louis: IN-gear for Careers; Katheryn Nelson, retired teacher and former manager with the Danforth Foundation Group; Carol Weisman, author, keynote speaker, and creator of the Board Builders organization.

Thanks also to current educators Tony Neal, principal at SIUE Charter School in East St. Louis Illinois; Ed Donnelly, teacher in the Lindbergh School District, Craig Larson, superintendent of the Rockwood School District; Jeff Spiegle, superintendent of the Ferguson-Florissant School District; Don Senti, superintendent of the Clayton School District all located in suburbs surrounding St. Louis, Missouri. The input offered by these readers provided valuable insights that helped produce this finished product.

I offer a special thank you to Laurie Mueller-Bevirt of Good Cause Communications for early editing and the cover design, and to Ted Wohlfarth, founder and executive director of EnTeam, and Bill Jenkins, author, retired teacher, and keynote speaker; both are friends and an inspiration for many of my "outlandish" ideas.

But mainly, I would like to thank the teachers, staff, and parents at Cahokia high school who were committed to putting in the extra effort required to implement the QUO Process and help improve the quality of education for our students. I would also like to thank the students for their increased attention to education. The efforts of everyone and the positive results achieved have inspired me to write this book for other educators. (Some of those results are shown below.)

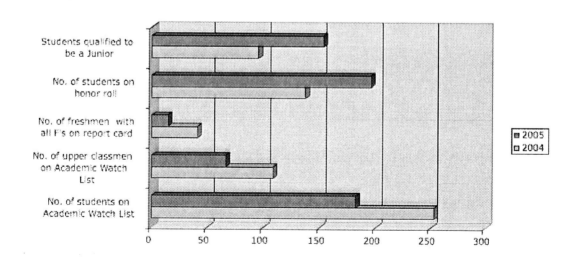

# Contents

# Forward

By Ted Wohlfarth
Executive Director of EnTeam

Why do so many students drop out of high school? What is needed to stop the exodus? What will make school engaging and worthwhile to students—especially the lowest performing students? How can teachers and administrators overcome the challenges they face and the frustration that drives too many teachers to burn out?

Dr. Ed Harris has pondered these questions for years as he transitioned from teacher to junior administrator to principal of high schools in Missouri and Illinois. He has studied the research and theories of leading educators. Out of these experiences and research, he has gathered the best practices into a unified and comprehensive plan for improving schools and has tested these ideas in schools where he has been principal. He has tested his ideas in diverse settings: inner-city schools with students from low-resource inner-city families, high-resource suburban families, and rural, farming families.

Over time, Dr. Harris has developed a comprehensive and unified plan for shattering the status quo and establishing a new QUO— a new level of quality, unity, and order. Ed has developed, tested, refined, and adapted his ideas to serve failing public schools. The result of those years of work is assembled and organized into a blueprint for making a school where everyone can succeed.

To help facilitate the QUO Process, Dr. Harris uses EnTeam strategies to reduce the frictions among people caused by restructuring a school system. These strategies help people to learn to win together on a win-win basis. They help people remember that change is easier when we bring out the best in each other. Together, the QUO Process and EnTeam strategies make possible Collaborative School Transformation.

Dr. Harris brings the perspective of a coach who has a plan for winning which he calls the QUO Process. He knows the problems that students face. He understands the subtleties and nuances that have defeated so many school districts. He knows that the plans have to be adjusted in the middle of the game because unexpected events will occur. Ed's motto is "the best laid plan is not good enough" —we have to improve based on the circumstances that arise and the available information that exists.

In Shattering Low Expectations, Dr. Harris does not mince words. He has strong opinions about the problems and the solutions. In fact, some readers may even find his observations and advice to be "politically incorrect." But, just like a coach with a plan for winning, he sometimes has to "talk tough."

You can actually feel the QUO Process if you walk through Cahokia High School while classes are in session. Rarely do you see a student in the hall. The structure of **order** is obvious as you walk. Less obvious is the **unity** among teachers, students, and families, but clues are there: Teachers planning together in the library. Parents who encourage their children to break the habits that had once pulled Cahokia High School down to the lowest levels of performance in Illinois. To see the **quality**, you have to look at the data and beyond: grades improving, test scores rising, curriculum in alignment with state requirements, students with failing grades "grounded" from field trips and attendance at extra curricular activities, and star athletes on the bench when their grades slip.

America needs answers! At a time when employers are demanding increasing levels of education, an academic underclass of students is being left behind. This underclass of students is unprepared to read and compute well enough to be employable in positions where they can earn a desirable wage. Many students that "drop out" leave school; others that drop out remain in school for the wrong reasons. Some people complain that in schools where academic achievement is high the struggling students are ignored; in schools where academic achievement is low some people complain that the high achievers are ignored. But whether drop-outs leave or stay or whether it is the achiever or struggler that is being ignored, the student's anger simmers just below the surface.

Dr. Harris believes that, "He who is willing to learn can learn, and those that seek to improve themselves ought to be nurtured and praised." Within the QUO Process, educators have the support and authority they need to run the school and teach. Parents have a clear role that they can fulfill without being expected to spend huge blocks of their precious time at school. And students understand that the adults are "in charge," both at home and at school, and that they have high expectations for student success.

# Preface

By Dr. Phil Hunsberger
Executive Director of the Metro East
Consortium for Child Advocacy
Co-Director of the International Network of Principals' Centers

Dr. Harris has devoted his professional life to extracting from his own experience what might transform schools on behalf of children. Though I seldom have faith in single dimensional prescriptions that suggest "do this and then do that," I find this book to be filled with a comprehensive lens for reform. I would suggest that readers embrace each chapter in that receptive state of – "Well I wonder if we ought to....?"

In August of 2003, I was invited to serve as an observer for a First Day Institute with the Cahokia High School staff. I was invited by Dr. Ed Harris who was in his first year as the principal of Cahokia High School; he invited me because of my role in the area. I am serving as the Executive Director of the Metro East Consortium of Child Advocacy (MECCA), a six-district partnership for professional development, of which Cahokia School District is a member. A major focus of MECCA is teaching and leading for social justice advocacy.

MECCA reaches to inspire educators toward instructional equity in an effort to ensure that all students experience high quality instruction in a positive learning environment, and that race is no longer a predictor of student outcome. Since I had already heard information regarding this "new" principal and some possibilities regarding the education of students at the high school, I was most interested in the invitation. Through this participation I received a meaningful introduction to the QUO Process. Now this book will also offer readers a comprehensive understanding of the elements of QUO Process. I was able to make comments to the staff as to my observation of the information shared on that day. Perhaps a review of these comments might serve well as a forward to this book.

As I listened to Dr. Harris and examined the notebook provided each teacher regarding the QUO process, it became clear that for this school: "It's not merely the old status quo!" Conditions were offered as to evidence of a new status quo that would be manifested in behavior and practice on behalf of the students of Cahokia High School. The "new status quo" would work to end the mythology of inferiority as a condition of human intellect, and in so doing, would begin to examine low academic achievement as experienced by many American-black high school students. The sad reality for these students is that they carry socialization that would suggest a certain limit to intellectual capability. In many ways, they cannot escape this socialization, thus leading to what Dr. Harris refers to in this book as "internalized self-doubt."

The new status quo, as suggested by the QUO Process, begins to develop a "counter-narrative"—something Theresa Perry calls for in her book, *Young, Gifted, and Black*. She writes that the construction of racial and gender identities that creates an ideology of inferiority must be confronted with a counter- or oppositional-narrative embedded in the day-to-day life of students. She also suggests that this counter-narrative be explicitly developed in the culture of school. Within this book practical ways to create a counter-narrative becomes a reality.

The QUO Process also puts in place the idea that the school is a place for learners, so that students, teachers, administrators, and even parents are included. Certainly much literature supports the idea of a community of learners as a meaningful description for a school. The QUO Process and this book help to make this idea both compelling and accomplishable. As evidenced in this book, the reader will find a number of suggestions that provide opportunities and activities for educators, students, and even parents to remain learners.

The QUO Process advocates and offers a meaningful network of communications. Regretfully, before Dr. Harris arrived, as is common for schools in urban settings, perceptions about Cahokia High School were disturbing, unpleasant, and misrepresented both students and teachers. However, perceptions to some people are realities. Therefore, those in urban schools could take steps to change negative perceptions. Dr. Harris promotes the idea of teachers contacting parents on a routine basis to share stories of success and potential rather than failure and futility. In addition, he was establishing with teachers and parents a disposition that would suggest that at Cahokia High School: "We are teaching Leaders!" Much of what could be done in schools is the nurturing of the irrefutable belief in the potential of all students to be successful learners.

The No Child Left Behind Act (NCLB) is certainly of righteous intention, and for me it suggests a Copernicus Act—one in which the center of the school universe is no longer the adult, but instead the student. As such we must begin to examine all that we have come to know as the status quo and seek evidence as to its efficacy on behalf of students. In so doing, we must be willing to thoughtfully scrutinize ideas that push us out of our comfort zones regarding teaching and learning. During that First Day Institute, Dr. Harris challenged his entire staff to think differently about what would constitute high expectations for students, and of equal importance, what would constitute pursuit of those expectations. The information contained in this text encourages educators to be relentless and committed in their efforts toward high expectations for students.

Finally, in this age of accountability, it is clear to me that QUO Process recognizes the importance of compliance to NCLB and focusing on what counts in regard to school improvement, and state and national assessments. This book and Dr. Harris' ideas center on the development of productive American citizens. In that effort, I'm sure the readers will encounter a number of ideas and notions that are most valuable for the development of character and integrity of young people—not such a bad focus for high schools in America.

# Introduction

By William Jenkins
Retired teacher, lecturer, and author

There is no problem in American education today that rivals that of bridging the gap between those who are doing well in our schools and those who are falling behind. It is a problem that is prevalent throughout the country and in practically every school district in America. Numerous educators and legislators have attempted to address the problem, but to date, none of those attempts have been able to close the gap in educational achievement between the best and the brightest and the rest of our students. In fact, in the last two decades, the gap that was once narrowing has started widening again.

To complicate the issue even further, the greatest numbers of those students who are falling behind are black. These are students who had been positioned to help erase some of the lingering effects of slavery and injustice and move closer to a society of full equality. They were to take the Civil Rights Movement to its next phase of fulfillment. But rather than taking advantage of this unprecedented opportunity, many of these students are shunning it by dropping out of school, or graduating with an inferior education and are in effect turning back the clock on their advancement toward full equality.

The No Child Left Behind Act (NCLB) is the latest legislative or administrative effort to address this issue. NCLB is more than just more educational legislation; it is a constitutional declaration. It is, in its own way, a test of whether our nation can ever live up to its advanced billing—a nation of free people with each having a chance to live out his or her full potential. We fought two wars on American soil—the Revolutionary War and the Civil War—to advance that belief. In a democracy such as ours, education is the key to freedom and fulfillment. If black people are ever to reach their full potential in America, they must be educated.

Unfortunately, you cannot educate people against their will. And many black children are coming to school lacking the will to dedicate themselves to the great task of catching up. And too often they find school settings and educators who are unprepared to change their minds and fashion them into students who can meet the challenges of these times.

Theories abound on how to effectively educate all of our children and to bridge the gap between those who are flourishing and those who are failing, but to date, few people and programs have been able to reverse this trend and show meaningful progress toward bridging the achievement gap. In fact, many of the theories in the public discussion will work in the right setting. Just about any sensible approach to education will work for those students who come to school well behaved, well prepared to be educated, and who are in tune with the plans and goals of education, especially if at their schools they encounter teachers who are just as eager to teach them as they are to learn. Neither is the case with black children and the other children who are being left behind; nor are their educators nearly as eager to teach them as are the educators are eager to teach those students attending high-achieving schools.

Since you can't educate people against their will, a great challenge for educators in a free society is to get people to do what they don't want to do when you know that in time they are going to wish they had done it. Those who come to the classroom entrenched in attitudes and behaviors that lead to failure need a special structure and approach to save them from themselves. One of the reasons that many of the programs designed to help the current group of students who are falling behind are ineffective is because they are not underpinned by a proper structure and are not protected by sufficient sovereignty.

Dr. Harris has developed an approach that has the structure and the internal controls necessary to achieve the goal of excellence. He calls his approach, the QUO Process. The QUO Process is just that, a process. Dr. Harris believes that structure is the foundation of educational success, especially with students who come from households and neighborhoods where structure is sorely missing. His process starts with the establishment of structure and begins to build the necessary components of education on that structure.

Dr. Harris has been in education for well over 20 years. He has spent the last 15 years in administration. From these positions he has implemented and refined the QUO Process. After working through the process time and time again, he has learned the problems that one will encounter working through that process and is sharing with educators in this book the process, the problems of implementing it, and methods of addressing those problems and achieving the goal of excellence that we all seek. This book shows educators how the path through the process is much smoother when it is maneuvered properly and certain measures are taken.

Dr. Harris believes that educational excellence is the result of hard work, and that work is more efficient and has better results when it is structured and organized. Students who fall behind in school are being outworked by those who are in front of them. Schools must put kids and teachers to work. They must specify what they do and measure the results often. And they must make adjustments when the results are not what they promise. They must insist that their raw material is capable of becoming the final product for which the public is paying. This will require that parents send them students who are willing to abide by the rules and do the work. Teachers and administrators must have the trust and authority to run the school like the business that it is so that they can get the results that the country claims it wants. In fact, that is really what NCLB says it wants. Schools have always done that for the students who are most successful; the QUO Process helps schools do the same for those students who have been the least successful.

Schools that are well structured will allow educators to unify around that structure. They can become one with the expectations and the goals of the school. Out of this structure and organization can come the quality education that all children deserve a chance to pursue. Dr. Harris believes in the QUO process. He believes deeply in a well-organized, well-run school where students are disciplined, teachers are dedicated, parents are involved, and everybody works hard. He believes that if schools nationally would adopt the QUO Process we would see a drastic improvement of the educational outcome of our students. It is that belief that led him to write this book and it is that belief that motivates him to do workshops wherever he is invited to explain the process to teachers and administrators. I have seen the QUO Process at work in Dr. Harris's schools and I am convinced that there is great potential in this process.

# Part One
# The Achievement Gap

Author's notes to readers:

1. *Many people label Americans with dark skin "African-Americans." However, it was centuries ago that our ancestors last saw Africa. Most of us know no one who has set foot in Africa. Many of our forefathers came to this continent before the founding of the United States. We were soldiers in the American Revolution. We are first and foremost Americans. The fact that our skin is darker than most is secondary to our identity as Americans. Therefore, where it is useful to identify us as anything more than Americans, I recommend the term American-black and use this term throughout this book.*

2. *In the pages ahead, some chapters have vignettes; the stories are true but the names are fictional to protect the confidentiality of the people and schools involved.*

# Chapter 1
# Don't Shoot the Messenger

*"It seems now in the year 2005 that a new kind of black parent has emerged. Many black parents today don't seem to want their children to be successful. They don't seem to care enough about their children's success to make the necessary sacrifices for that success to happen. It almost seems that today's black parents don't really care about their children; they appear to want their children to be inferior. And this distresses me."*

William Jenkins, *Recipe For Raising Thugs*—How to Rear Inferior Black Children.

### Sasafrazz's Mad Mama:

As I walked toward the main office foyer, the voices I heard became louder. I recognized the voices of two of my assistant principals. When I opened the foyer door, I saw a large American-black woman. The mother wore loose-fitting clothing, a black wig of wavy hair that fell to her shoulders, and glasses that looked too tight against her round face. She stood firmly and asserted defense of her child with abrupt gesticulations with her large arms.

I interrupted and said, *"I'm the principal. May I help you?"*

The American-white male assistant principal departed to tend to other business.

*"I wish somebody would help me; I'm sick and tired of that English teacher picking on my baby,"* said Sasafrazz's mother.

*"Would you like to step into my office so you can tell me what happened?"* I asked.

*"I don't need to step in no office. I just need to go find that teacher and give her a piece of my mind,"* she said.

I folded my hands in front and spoke to her in the softest voice that I could muster and asked, *"What happened?"*

In a loud voice, the mother explained, *"That white teacher keeps making my baby write her papers over. Every time she turns it in, that white teacher makes her do it again. Now this is the fourth time that she has had to do it over."*

I sensed that as the mother spoke, she became more agitated.

The American-black assistant, Mrs. Stanstrong, said, *"Mrs. Washington, Sasafrazz knows that Mrs. Charles is strict and that she requires all of the students to rewrite papers until they get them right. Don't you want Sasafrazz to learn to write correctly?"*

*"I go to college myself and I helped Saz write the paper the last time and she even thought of some things that I didn't know to put in the paper. That white teacher still made her write it again. I think that woman don't like my child."*

I tried to calm the mother and asked her what college she attended.

*"I go to the junior college,"* she said.

*"Are you taking English Composition?"* I asked.

*"Yes, and the teacher says that I writes pretty good but she always manages to find something wrong and makes me rewrite some of my papers."*

*"How does that make you feel when you have to write papers a second or third time?"* I asked.

*"I hate it,"* she said.

I was positioning her for "the moment of understanding" when I asked her, *"Do you think that you learned what you needed to know to prepare you for college English Composition when you were in high school?"*

She shook her head and said, *"I went to this high school and they didn't teach me nothing here neither."*

I smiled inwardly as she moved into the gambit that I had set.

*"Then do you wish that the teachers would have made you rewrite some of those high school papers so that it wouldn't be so difficult for you at the junior college now?"* I asked.

*"Them teachers didn't teach us black kids nothing. They don't want us to be smart,"* she said.

I realized that she still had no clue as to what I was attempting to explain. I decided to be more direct and said, *"The teacher is taking the time to teach Sasafrazz now so that by the time she goes to college, writing a composition will come as second nature. Because of what Mrs. Charles is doing, Sasafrazz will be able to write as well as most of the students her age and better than some."*

The three of us continued to talk for a while. The longer we talked, the more Mrs. Washington calmed. Finally, I suggested that she talk to Mrs. Charles tomorrow, after a cooling off period. I explained to Mrs. Washington that Sasafrazz must understand that getting smart requires hard work and that she should not rest unless she has done her very best on every assignment in every class.

Unfortunately the messenger is often crucified when the receivers of the message do not like the message, the tone of the message, or the looks of the messenger. Frequently the receivers of a painful message find a multiplicity of ways to discredit and demonize the messenger. Often, conversation concerning new and better ways to accomplish this becomes more of a focus than discussing and exploring ways to address the real issue.

Sasafrazz's mother, Mrs. Washington, did not like the message being sent by Sasafrazz's teacher. The teacher was simply trying to help Sasafrazz become a better writer. Mrs. Washington was defending Sasafrazz when she may have better served her daughter's future by insisting that she follow the teacher's direction rather than caving in to Sasafrazz's complaining because she had to do extra writing.

## Message to Heed:

Fact—American-black students are failing to reach benchmarks on state and national standardized tests. These tests were created to assess how much individual students know of the agreed-upon body of knowledge necessary to prosper in mainstream American society.

The test scores in almost all schools with 10 percent or more American-black students reveal that too many American-black students are scoring lower, much lower than all other races of students in America. It is not uncommon to discover that American-black students graduating from high school score less than American-white seventh-graders on math and geography tests. A difference in comprehension is also true in writing, reading, and social studies. Politicians, business people, and educators have termed this phenomenon "**The Achievement Gap**."

This gap has been discovered in schools where the American-black students are in the minority, the majority, where they are from low-resource families, from high-resource families, where they are catholic, or protestant.

## The Gatekeepers

A residual effect of the gap is that employers, admissions officers at colleges, and other gatekeepers for advancement may be hard-pressed in their screening duties to allow American-black applicants to be chosen over candidates of other races because of the stigma of this achievement gap. American-black gatekeepers are not immune to this kind of thinking; they have been exposed to the same negative message so there may be some doubt in their minds as they interview the American-black candidates. A person with tremendous ability might get passed over for progressive advancement because the gatekeepers unwittingly allow knowledge of the existence of the gap to negatively influence their decisions when the candidate for the position is American-black.

**Those educators that can understand what it could mean for the future of America if this trend continues and want to be part of the solution rather than part of the problem should continue reading.**

## Swimming Upstream to the "Green" Mainstream

In America, most children are sent to public schools to learn the information that might put them on a path to success in mainstream America, now becoming known as the **"Green Culture."**

Those Americans of Irish, Italian, British, Asian, Latino, Jamaican, Spanish, and any other descent have independent cultures within their families and communities, but their level of prosperity rests with how well and to what degree they can internalize the mainstream American culture. The parents and adults in each ethnic family that best impress upon their children the significance of mastering the language, behaviors, and skills that are held in high regard in mainstream American culture will have the surest and most consistent avenues toward success; it is no different for American-black people. If American-black children want to have a piece of the green culture rock, most of them will have to get it by achieving an education.

## The Right Stuff

Unfortunately, volumes of data show that at-risk students, especially American-black students, are simply not learning enough of the "right stuff" in public schools to prepare for the high-stakes tests facing students throughout the country. This lack of preparation will eventually impact the students' earning power and narrow their choices beyond high school. Almost all of the low achievers will endure poverty and extremely limited opportunities. The realities that accompany this condition usually create volatile hostilities within many low achievers. Lessons from history reveal that a poor, hostile populous with external similarities such as color, religion, and race, that are different from the majority population, creates a very negative psychological situation.

**Whatever criteria are used to determine selection will have its opponents and proponents. Educators, beyond personal feelings concerning the effectiveness or non-effectiveness, rightness or wrongness of the testing criteria, must in the final analysis discover which criteria will be used to determine which students will be advanced, accepted, or selected. Then, educators must find ways to help students gain the knowledge, skills, and attitudes necessary to be able to meet or exceed the benchmarks.** In this way educators, teach the right stuff and help students progress along avenues of interest as they enter post-secondary life.

## Authentic vs. Academic

Among low-achieving American-black students, many reject learning and intimidate and harass students who do earn high marks. The harassing students often bully the achieving American-black students, sometimes calling them "Uncle Tom," and sometimes actually causing physical harm. The accusation many achieving American-blacks dread most is that academic achievement equals "trying to be white."

American-blacks attempting to succeed in school are merely imitating whites; the insidious psychology behind this thinking implies that only American-whites can learn academic information. By this way of thinking, one cannot be authentically black and academically successful simultaneously. This worldview also implies something is wrong when American-blacks use American-white people as role models, heroes, or mentors. Furthermore,

> American-blacks attempting to succeed in school are merely imitating whites; the insidious psychology behind this thinking implies that only American-whites can learn academic information.

American-blacks should avoid having American-white friends. This psychology further implies that a white person is weak-minded when it comes to real life and earthy existence, un-cool, and out-of-touch with reality—the consummate nerd. This line of thinking leads to, and even requires, separatist, segregationist thinking and behaviors.

Using if-then logic, the people that forward such psychology believe that American-black students should not find value in learning academic information, should reject anything advocated by whites, should avoid all cordial relationships with whites, and should embrace all black people and their ideas and behaviors, even when wrong. This thinking devastates American-black students and often blocks the pursuit of academic achievement. Many achieving American-black students seldom want their achievement to become common knowledge. They realize that to gain notoriety for smartness brings ridicule and contempt from many of their American-black student peers.

# Chapter 2
## Insights into the Low Academic Achievement
## of American-Black Students

*"To help unmotivated students, Brophy (1986) suggested a process called attribution retraining, which involved modeling, socialization, and practice exercises. The goals of attribution retraining are to help students (1) concentrate on the task rather than becoming distracted by fear of failure; (2) respond to frustration by retracing their steps to find mistakes or figuring out alternative ways of approaching a problem instead of giving up; and (3) attribute their failures to insufficient effort, lack of information, or reliance on ineffective strategies rather than to lack of ability."*

*Bill Macdonald, Ed. D.  Principal N.O. Nelson Elementary School in Edwardsville, Illinois;"Today's Schools" (January/February 2005)*

### "Success Enough for Me"

The teacher sent her to the office because she had been absent more than 30 school days. The teacher indicated on the written referral, the student handed to me that Deshonda seemed to attend most frequently on Wednesday. I reviewed Deshonda's attendance record and noticed a peculiar pattern. Indeed, Deshonda seemed to attend school once a week, almost always on Wednesday. Upon further investigation, I discovered that Deshonda was 17 years old with a birthday coming in a few weeks.

I asked Deshonda, *"I notice on the attendance report you come to school only once a week but I see you just about everyday here at school, why is that?"* Deshonda said, *"I come almost every day but I don't usually go to classes."*

*"Why do you come every day if you don't attend class?"*

*"I ride the bus to school; I see my friends, eat breakfast, eat lunch then walk home."*

*"Why don't you just see your friends in the evening at home?"*

*"I don't have time. My momma will watch my kids in the morning but she goes out in the evenings and she does not allow me to have visitors when she ain't home."*

*"Why do you eat lunch here? Most students would go out to lunch if they had the opportunity."*

*"I get free breakfast and lunch when I eat here; you can't beat free."*

For the first time I noticed that Deshonda was pregnant. I asked, *"Are you saying that you already have two children?"*

She smiled proudly, shook her head, held her stomach with both hands and said, *"Yeah, and it's going to be three in about three more months."*

I asked, *"I want you to be successful but what is your plan to care for your children when you don't have an education?"*

*"I'm gonna be just like my momma; I'll take ADC."*

*"Aid for Dependant Children is not very much money on which to raise a family."*

*"Well, my momma already got me on LINC and I get money from the state. My momma gives me half the money we get for me being designated special education and with my third baby I'll be getting about $1,000 a month ADC. My Living Independently Now Center (LINC) qualification gives me access to certain foods for the baby and me at the supermarket and in a few months I'll be eligible to get my own place with section eight housing. That's success enough for me."*

## Who is Most At-Risk?

American-black girls are definitely at risk, especially when they become teenage mothers, but even more at risk are American-black boys. According to Rosa A. Smith in her book, Saving Black Boys: The Elusive Promise of Public Education:

*"Among the many children in America who are at risk and likely to lack success in school, most often because they lack authentic educational opportunities, the African-American male student stands alone in terms of the accumulation of negative factors affecting his future. The evidence is startling, and the sum of all these negative factors is alarming."*

# SAD, SAD STATS

*"Today, education is perhaps the most important function of state and local governments. It is a principal instrument in awakening the child to cultural values, in preparing him for later professional training, and in helping him adjust normally to his environment...it is doubtful that any child may reasonably be expected to succeed in life if he is denied the opportunity of an education."*

*Chief Justice Earl Warren, Supreme Court's Brown vs. Board of Education decision in 1954.*

These remarks are as relevant today as when said by Chief Justice Warren some 50 years ago. According to *The American Prospect*, American-black boys in 2000-2001 made up 8.6 percent of national public school enrollments. However, they constituted:

- 20 percent of those classified as mentally retarded
- 21 percent of those classified as emotionally disturbed
- 12 percent of those classified with a specific learning disability
- 15 percent of those placed in special education

**Twice as many black boys are in special education as black girls**, a fact that rules out heredity and home environment as primary causes and highlights school factors. American adults must confront the devastating condition of American-black boys. While between 25 percent and 30 percent of America's teenagers, including recent immigrants, fail to graduate from high school with a regular high school diploma, the dropout rate for American-black males in many metropolitan areas is 50 percent. It gets worse, nationally:

- 86 percent of white females receive high school diplomas
- 80 percent of white males receive high school diplomas
- 61 percent of black females receive high school diplomas
- 50 percent of black males receive high school diplomas

Despite representing only 8.6 percent of public school enrollments, black boys comprise 22 percent of those expelled from school and 23 percent of those suspended from school. Further, 105 out of every 100,000 whites are incarcerated, but 350 out of every 100,000 blacks are jailed. More American-black males receive the GED in prison than graduate from college.

> **More American-black males receive the GED in prison than graduate from college.**

According to the 2000 census, 24.7 percent of black youths aged 16 to 19 neither work nor attend school—nearly twice the national averages for this age group and six times the national unemployment rate.

Data demonstrates that schools have been relatively unsuccessful in saving American-black males from a tragic existence. Futurist Harold Hodgkinson in the 1900's wrote that the graduates of 2000 would have more knowledge available to them in high school than their grandparents had available to them in a lifetime. The body of knowledge available to students has doubled four times since 1988. Schools have to find better ways of sorting the knowledge and getting the most important knowledge to the students in more effective and efficient ways. As you'll see later in this book, the QUO Process specifically aids in this endeavor.

People need education more desperately than ever as the world heads into the 21st century. Currently only 6 percent or fewer people find assembly line jobs. Ninety percent of current jobs consist of service and 95 percent involve distributing information about service or information about something else. Almost every job will require some job-specific training beyond high school. Many jobs currently go unfilled because of a lack of entry-level candidates.

American-black youngsters are in serious trouble because they have been allowed to run amuck, and most educators, community members, American-black care-givers, and parents have not intervened. American-black adults have not held American-black young people to a high enough standard. This low level of expectation manifests itself in schools. American-black students regularly find themselves at the bottom rung in every academic area measured.

Consequently, typical American-black underachievement reinforces one of the worst stereotypes about American-blacks: "Blacks just aren't book smart." Meanwhile, another generation of American-black students drifts through school without acquiring skills and knowledge necessary to negotiate mainstream culture. The old racist joke, "If you want to hide something from black people, put it in a book" almost rings true when one reviews the data about American-black academic achievement, yet not enough American-black people seem to have a sense of urgency about this.

According to research accumulated by Abigail and Stephan Thernstrom in their book No Excuses, large percentages of American-black students fall below basic in all core curriculum areas. The National Assessment of Educational Progress (NAEP) results show that in five of seven subjects tested, over 50 percent of American-black students score below basic as compared to less than 20 percent of American-white students. Only in writing do less than 50 percent of American-black students score below basic. Nearly half of all Asians and 40 percent of whites rank in the top two categories in reading while less than 20 percent of American-black students rank that high. While 3.4 percent of American-Asians and 3.0 percent of American-whites score at the advanced level in science, only 0.1 percent of American-blacks score that high.

The facts cause even more alarm when the scrutiny deepens. In math, only 0.2 percent of American-blacks score at the advanced level while American-whites have 11 times that amount and American-Asians score 37 times higher. With so few American-blacks acquiring superb skills by the end of high school, the pool of those destined for roles as American professionals and business elite grows excruciatingly small. Up to 1988, the gap in reading improved but slippage occurred in the 1990s. Since 1999, according to standardized tests, the average American-black student knows less science than 90 percent of American-white students. The gap between American-whites and American-blacks in math and science continues to widen.

## Skill Scarcity

The presence of American-blacks in engineering, medicine, and Silicon Valley computer wizardry is scarce because American-black students know so little math and science.

The usual educational strategies—more money, smaller classes, standards, testing, or accountability—will not heal the above wounds. Something different has to be done. This problem does not exist in isolation. It occurs whether the American-black students come from high- or low-resource homes, whether they live in the city or the suburbs, or whether they attend schools where they are the majority or the minority.

If low representation of American-blacks in high-level positions and influential professions continues, American-blacks will be locked in second-class citizenship for an indeterminate future. This unfortunate situation will not resolve itself by affirmative action initiatives alone. American-black adults must demand that American-black students get smarter faster, and they must require that American-black students start getting smarter today.

The Thernstroms point to the research questioning that perhaps growing up in a single, female-headed household affects academic performance. Such family structures correlate highly with lower educational attainment and more behavioral and psychological problems for the children. The racial group with the lowest proportion of students from single parent families (American-Asians) has less discipline problems and higher academic performance. The racial group with the highest proportion of students from single parent families (American-blacks) has more discipline problems and lower academic performance.

The Thernstroms also explain that many American-black students consider watching TV their "social homework." They think that watching programs with predominately American-black casts or content helps American-black students "stay cool." Therefore, American-blacks spend five hours or more each evening watching TV and 15 percent less time on homework than American-white students do. Twenty percent less likely to finish assignments than American-white students, American-blacks reported doing 3.9 hours of schoolwork per week; American-whites say that they spend 5.4 hours per week on schoolwork—40 percent more than American-blacks. American-Asians report that they spend 7.5 hours per week on schoolwork, 40 percent more than whites, but nearly twice as much as American-blacks.

But most distressing, many American-black students and their parents have joined with a larger contingency of American-blacks who are embedded in an "**oppositional culture**" hostile to academic excellence. They feel racism is ineradicable from American society and conclude that educational success will not pay. Therefore, meeting the demands of school marks an American-black as selling out. In reality however, in a study of Americans age 25 and older, those that leave school before ninth grade earn only 33.3 percent of what those who completed a bachelor's degree achieve, and with each step up the educational ladder, the earnings disparity rises.

> A portion of the solution to the achievement gap lies in cultural attitudes toward education.

According to research cited by the National Center for Education Statistics, and the *Digest of Education Statistics*, over a working life, Americans, regardless of race, that graduate college will earn $850,000 more than those that drop out of high school. Those that earn a graduate degree earn $1.7 million more than will dropouts. This data suggests that the choices of behaviors, attitudes, and expectations that American-black students and their parents have toward education will have a dynamic impact on a student's possibilities in school and beyond. A portion of the solution to the achievement gap lies in cultural attitudes toward education.

## Is Poverty the Cause?

According to Michael A. Fletcher's article, "Indiana Schools Shrink Black-White Divide: A Focus on Attitudes Raises Attitudes in Scores," Washington Post, February 21, 2002, poverty does not explain the achievement gap. American-black students that come from poverty families still score significantly lower on standardized tests when compared to American-white students that come from poverty families (as determined by the federal school meals program). The education level of the parents does not explain the achievement gap either. Although the disparity in academic performance between American-white and American-black students does widen as the level of education of the parents increases, American-white children with high school-educated parents will perform better than American-black children with high school-educated parents. As the level of education increases for both sets of parents, the performance gaps between the American-white and American-black students increase.

Fletcher further suggests that moving to the suburbs is not an answer to the achievement gap for American-blacks. The data reveals that American-blacks living in the suburbs score better than urban American-blacks, but suburban American-whites also outscore urban American-whites. When American-blacks who live in the suburbs compete with their American-white classmates, the whites perform better.

In her book *A Framework for Understanding Poverty*, Ruby Payne, supported by data collected by the U.S. Bureau of Census, attempts to explain the culture of poverty. She makes it clear that poverty is not something that is owned by one race of people. Even though there are not as many American-blacks in poverty (3,492,000) as there are American-whites in poverty (7,527,000), the percentage of the American-black population that is in poverty is much higher (30.2 percent) than the percentage of American-whites in poverty (13.4 percent) and higher than the percentage of people in poverty in the total population of America (13.4 percent).

The poverty line in 2001 was considered to be $18,104 for a family of four. Payne makes the argument that people living in poverty have a common way of viewing life that is different from people living above the poverty line. In the vignette at the beginning of this chapter, Deshonda's view of success was not the same as someone from mainstream America. In her community, neighborhood, and family, Deshonda's concept of success is probably more like those around her than it is different. Educators must keep this in mind when teaching in a school that serves large numbers of youngsters and their families that are living below the poverty line.

Students living in poverty often have a worldview that is limited by the economic conditions under which they live. They rarely have the resources to see a wider view of what is possible or available in America and the world. Even when they do get exposure, maybe from television, movies, or other forms of media they might decide that the possibilities are there for others but are not available to them. Payne suggests that the 16.3 percent of Americans living below the poverty line have many of the same issues and concerns regardless of race.

*However, from the perspective of American-black students the issue of race is real, and it is something that they all must face. This must be acknowledged if a positive impact on their education is to be made.* Consequently, students in families that are living below the poverty line and are also American-black must adjust to being black in America *and* being poor. American-black students that are fortunate enough to be members of families with resources above the poverty line often feel that they still must face reactions by the white majority to their blackness. Both of the psychologies, poverty and being black in America, help pull or lull American-black students into an achievement gap and create a challenge for educators when interacting with American-black students.

# THREE MAIN CAUSES OF THE ACHIEVEMENT GAP

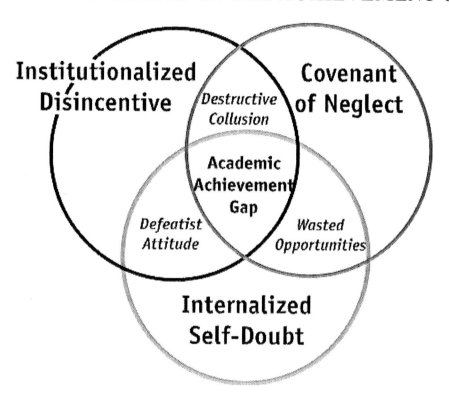

The main three reasons for the achievement gap are:

1. **Covenant of Neglect:** Many people, both American-black and American-white, have been successful at joining within covenants of neglect. These covenants are secret or unspoken agreements among people within institutions, families and communities, not to intervene to address institutionalized disincentive and internalized self-doubt.

2. **Institutionalized Disincentive:** Systems of institutionalized disincentive may exist in organizations, families, and youth culture. In many of these three entities, established or ritualized deterrents and hindrances, conscious or unconscious, exist to discourage American-black children. While repression is often manifested for American-black youngsters in various institutions of society, the network of institutional structures, policies, and practices that create advantages and benefits for American-white youngsters are often invisible to them, or are considered "rights"

available to everyone, as opposed to privileges denied to American-black youths.

3. **Internalized Self-Doubt:** Destructive feelings of self-doubt are often cultivated and transmitted by institutions and American-black families and internalized by some American-black children. Within this feeling of self-doubt many American-black youngsters become entrapped in attitudes of uncertainty, disbelief, with reservations and misgivings about themselves. Often, young American-black people turn this negative self-suspicion inward and direct it at each other.

# THE PATHOLOGY OF SUBORDINATION

A component of the covenant of neglect is the "pathology of subordination." **This pathology of subordination is a mentality that invites people to believe that American-black people should remain "in their place"**—a place deeply planted in the psyche of many American people where American-blacks occupy a subordinate position to American-whites in society. Further, many people believe that this position of subordination should be maintained eternally or at least indefinitely.

**From the American-White Perspective:** American-whites who embrace the pathology of subordination are not interested in the academic improvement of American-black students. American-whites who embrace the pathology of subordination do not believe that American-black students can achieve or they simply do not want them to achieve; in the words of President G. W. Bush, "a soft bigotry exists in America." Soft bigots do not support holding American-black students to high standards partially because they do not want their promotion of the idea of black inadequacy to be proven wrong.

American-whites who embrace the pathology of subordination have no desire to motivate American-black students and do not want others to motivate them either. This perspective actually has two components: **the missionary approach** and **the pragmatic approach**. The missionary approach is explained well by Eric Cooper in the second chapter of the book, *Teaching All The Children*, where he explains that some people believe that American-black people "have fallen victim to negative social engineering and that those children who have been challenged by poverty and who lack European ancestors just do not have the capacity for the level of learning that might lead to 'rich and powerful' careers. Why raise the poor non-white's aspirations through social activist policies only to see them dashed by innate cognitive limitations?"

American-whites who embrace the pathology of subordination fight against any people, plans, programs, or processes that would place American-black students into positions that would lead them to academic success. Those who take the pragmatic approach, as explained at a pre-publishing meeting by author Carol Weisman (2005), "believe that resources, jobs, places in college, places in the military, job promotions, and career positions are finite and therefore must be protected for white people. Teaching blacks strategies that will help them gain qualifications to vie for the resources would, in this line of thinking, make less of the resources available to whites and the children of whites."

**From the American-Black Perspective:** American-black adults who embrace the pathology of subordination are not interested in doing what is necessary to help American-black students improve academically. This attitude usually takes one of two forms:

**oppositional** and **disengaged**. Those who follow the oppositional approach refuse to do well in school and on standardized tests; they associate school and tests with whiteness and they resent and reject whiteness at every opportunity; they see themselves as rebels, or warriors against whites and their privilege. Those who follow the disengaged approach use disincentive; they don't want their children to "get smarter than the parents."

There are at least two reasons American-black adults who embrace the pathology of subordination avoid responsibility and hard work.

1. One reason is because of the personal improvement that it would require. Learning in school brings too much of a personal investment and might mean that accountability standards will be expected of American-black adults (teachers and parents).

2. A second reason is that they fear that the rewards other groups of people receive when they embrace the mainstream culture will continue to be withheld from American-black people and they do not want to be made fools; they do not want their hearts or the hearts of their children to continue to be broken.

Each time an American-black person who meets the requirements of mainstream culture is denied acceptance, admission, promotion, or advancement, **reasons for non-compliance are reinforced**. Each time an American-black person is advanced without meeting the requirements of the mainstream, non-compliance is also reinforced. American-black adults who embrace the pathology of subordination realize that they are not held to the same expectations as everyone else; they know that expectations have their costs and if met can possibly bring excruciating disappointments.

Rewards have come to American-black adults who embrace the pathology of subordination, without the responsibility of accountability. They have received jobs, free food, special attention, and recognition without earning it or engaging in the rigor necessary to meet the standards of credibility that usually precede such rewards. American-black adults who embrace the pathology of subordination and their allies (American-whites who embrace the pathology of subordination) regularly applaud American-black young people for minimal production or achievement. This of course has been sending the wrong message to American-black students and has hampered their academic development.

**From the American-Black Student Perspective:** American-black students who embrace the pathology of subordination when offered the choice between low-level courses or challenging options consistently choose the less challenging alternatives; but they seek and even expect to receive the same praise and privilege of those students that take and achieve in the higher-level courses. The American-black students that embrace the pathology of subordination are satisfied with passing or simply attending classes. They do not value meeting standards or demonstrating proficiency. In many schools American-black students who embrace the pathology of subordination get attention, rewards, accolades, and even privileges without meeting the accountability standards that are required by other students and when they do not get what they want they play the "race card" and point to racism as their nemesis.

In effect, American-white adults, American-black adults, and American-black students that embrace the pathology of subordination are in alliance producing and enabling apathy and continued low achievement among American-black students. American-whites who embrace the pathology of subordination cultivate the paternalism of keeping American-blacks dependent and under-qualified for most leadership or professional positions in mainstream America; American-blacks who embrace the pathology of subordination are willing to pay the price of second class citizenship in the eyes of those in the mainstream as long as they are allowed to enjoy the absence of responsibility while receiving indulgences from their American-white allies. Those within this alliance, American-whites and American-blacks, most often work independently, but join forces when necessary to discredit or verbally attack anyone that attempts to bring accountability, standards, and therefore equity to American-black students. Those in the alliance may belong because of different reasons, but nonetheless belong just the same.

The pathology of subordination has held prominence in the mentality that drives some of American policy, and in the culture and climate of many public schools. According to Eric Cooper in the book, *Teaching All the Children,*

*"Schools, rather than functioning as the great equalizer, tend to both reflect and replicate social-class structures and societal biases ... the end result: families in the top 25 percent of income send 86 percent of their children to college; while families in the bottom 20 percent send 4 percent of their children to college."*

Those that accept the pathology of subordination not only do not want American-black students to be put on the path to success, they also have a deep distaste for American-blacks that have moved into the mainstream.

When American-blacks *do* internalize the language, demeanor, and etiquette of mainstream culture, many times there is a backlash from American-blacks who support the pathology of subordination. They may refer to the American-blacks that internalize mainstream culture as sell-outs.

The American-whites who support the pathology of subordination refer to the American-blacks that internalize the mainstream as either "uppity blacks" or sarcastically as "the whitest black people" that they have ever seen. Both blacks and whites who support the pathology of subordination do all within their power to repress, hold back, and stifle the advancement of mainstream American-blacks. When people with such attitudes have influence over American-black students, the result is academic and psychological devastation.

# INSTITUTIONALIZED DISINCENTIVE

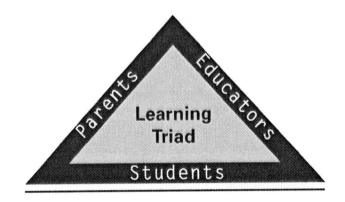

26

**When disincentive is institutionalized within schools, the repetitive message of the inferiority of American-blacks is commonplace.** When institutionalized disincentive is allowed to exist within schools because of the existence of a covenant of neglect by the adults involved, it causes a destructive collusion between some within the "Learning Triad"—students, educators, parents and community members.

This can result in caustic sometimes even vicious, negative complicity. In schools where disincentive is institutionalized, people within the Learning Triad that are so inclined also embrace attitudes of disincentive and direct them toward youngsters who are struggling academically.

In schools where institutionalized disincentive exists, the curriculum ignores, minimizes, or distorts the history of black people, or it overplays the contributions and accomplishments of black people. This demonstrates a lack of interest in the culture of black people or an unbalanced approach to the American-black experience in the Western world.

The results of the first approach are that guidelines for admission to many programs are designed in such a way that it is highly unlikely that American-black students have been exposed to the experiences necessary to qualify. The message from this approach is clear: American-black students are not appreciated, unwanted, and seen as academically inferior.

The results of the second approach are that American-black people give themselves an inflated, elevated, false sense of sophistication. The message here is clear as well: American-blacks do not have to be held to the same accountability measures as other people.

# INTERNALIZED SELF-DOUBT

After hearing these messages and seeing plenty of fabricated evidence that supports such thinking, **many American-black students begin to *believe* they cannot succeed.** They internalize self-doubt and look into the mirror noticing a person doomed to failure staring back at them. Many individual American-black students project these negative feelings about themselves onto others within their race. Students who attend school where an internalized disincentive environment exists then internalize the oppression and take on a defeatist attitude; they have a fatalistic, despondent, pessimistic viewpoint, outlook, and approach to life. Such students learn to believe that American-black students cannot achieve academically; they believe that American-black students are not "book-smart," cannot do math or construct an appropriate expository written piece.

Some people believe that the Pygmalion Effect, where the American-black students meet the low expectations of their academic skills, is a major cause of the low academic achievement of American-black students. When American-black students internalize self-doubt and the covenant of neglect allows it to continue, many opportunities that American-black students could have gained are wasted, emaciated, or withered, and chances, breaks, and prospects are exhausted.

Adult stakeholders, within and those surrounding institutions where internalized self-doubt and institutionalized disincentive exist, often choose not to address either problem. They sometimes pretend that one or both of these problems do not exist and in this denial allow the problems to proliferate. Educators locked in covenants of neglect rarely confront systems of disincentive that they know exist and few American-black educators confront or even acknowledge the existence of internalized self-doubt. Some American-blacks have spent more energy complaining about racism than they have on the work that needs to be done to address internalized self-doubt.

> **Some American-blacks have spent more energy complaining about racism than they have on the work that needs to be done to address internalized self-doubt.**

However, other American-black leaders argue that until the internalized self-doubt that exists within many American-black students is addressed, low academic achievement will continue even if racism lay dormant. It is clear that when internalized self-doubt meets institutionalized disincentive inside a school where covenants of neglect exist, gaps in achievement cannot be avoided.

## Addicted to Failure?

According to William Jenkins in his book *Educating African-American Children*, from the standpoint of parents and educators, only one of two ways exist to view the documentation of low achievement and performance of American-black students:

> *"Either American-black children are genetically inferior, or parents and educators have been doing something wrong in reference to the development of American-black children."*

> **These failing students detract from their own communities and ultimately they threaten the entire American political and economic system.**

Due to internalized self-doubt, large numbers of American-black students purposely adopt the kind of behaviors that lead to low achievement and failure, and many American-black communities and schools have enabled this.

American-black students that embrace failure consistently use inappropriate behaviors that are in direct opposition to what they perceive as being characteristic of "white society," such as being loud, obnoxious, violent, aggressive, and disruptive. Consequently, American-black students that constantly choose to use failure-yielding behaviors often become deliberate nuisances at school. These failing students detract from their own communities and ultimately they threaten the entire American political and economic system.

Students of any race that are addicted to failure should be confronted, but American-black students addicted to failure pose the most critical problem today.

When a student consistently displays three or more of the following behaviors, it is evidence that the student is probably addicted to failure:

- Has frequent mood swings and is easily agitated on Friday
- Regularly arrives at school on Monday angry with other students amid rumors that a fight will occur during the day because of problems over the weekend

- Often finds ways to escalate simple misbehavior into behavior that brings more serious consequences
- Between long periods of extreme ineffectiveness and failure to turn in schoolwork, he or she, without any apparent explanation, has occasional grade level-appropriate academic performance
- Demonstrates evasiveness or over-generalizes during conversations about the ineffectiveness of his or her academic performance
- Uses an assortment of methods to block positive, proactive, cordial, and collaborative contact between parents and educators
- Has grandiose and unrealistic ideas about a professional career that does not correspond to his or her real life behaviors and academic performance
- Has more personal crises and difficulties with staff members than most students
- Is quick to join fracases and inappropriate behaviors initiated by others
- Has explosive reactions on a regular basis to minor corrective instructions given by staff members

## The "Bad Apple Syndrome"

Even more disturbing, a Bad Apple Syndrome has developed where American-black students addicted to failure-yielding behaviors negatively affect the academic achievement of other students. In the words of William Jenkins:

*"We must think of schools as gardens and any good gardener knows that it is counter-productive to tend the weeds and leave the flowers to grow on their own. Flowers will tolerate weeds but weeds will not tolerate flowers. Weeds destroy flowers but flowers do not harm weeds. If weeds are allowed to flourish, the flowers are choked."*

Some achieving students, both American-blacks and American-whites, often aspire to connect socially with American-black students that choose failure. Their failures set them apart as "cool rebels," young people with poignant insights beyond current mainstream understanding.

Students who voluntarily connect with students choosing academic failure sometimes move into the realm of defiant gangster rap music with its funky rhythms, profanity-laced lyrics and the "hip" and raunchy streetwise slang. This is usually the expression and language currency of students that choose to use inappropriate behaviors. Tragically, not long after making this "connection to cool," many achieving students begin to experience a slide toward failure, and some slide faster than others.

American-black students who embrace failure promote constant rebellion against what they perceive as a "mainly for whites" society; **their real rebellion however is against compliance to structure.** They defy authority and incessantly demand that those around them adopt anti-white and anti-establishment attitudes. **They associate almost everything that represents civility—making good grades, manners, character, and appropriate etiquette— with whiteness or establishment-compatible behavior, therefore making it "un-cool" and consequently undesirable.** Other students who do not follow the lead of these rebellious American-black students quickly find themselves ostracized from acceptance within "circles of coolness."

Circumstances force some students, including achieving American-blacks, to interact socially and academically with students that constantly choose to use failure-yielding behaviors. Many have the misfortune of riding the bus or sitting in classrooms with them. This occurs especially where progressive schools have elected to divest themselves of basic skills classes.

As explained by the late Greg Freeman, deceased columnist for the St. Louis Post Dispatch newspaper, **endeavoring American-black students labor under constant surveillance by the "Soul Patrol."** These roaming, ever-vigilant American-black students who pursue failure, spy relentlessly to catch endeavoring American-black students failing to act anti-white or "black enough."

Other American-blacks also force endeavoring American-black students into "bonds of personalism," a term coined by Marion Orr of Boston University. Loosely translated, the term means that in order for a black person to gain full acceptance within the black enclave and earn recognition as a "true" black person, he or she **must** support other blacks, American or foreign, even if they constantly choose behaviors that lead to social or academic failure. Failure to conform to bonds of personalism or earning the label of derision by the Soul Patrol brings that dreaded sobriquet, "trying to be white." For many American-black students, this "put-down" hurts worse than "nigger" or any other slur with racial connotations.

As related to the achievement gap, achieving students will tolerate students that embrace failure-yielding behaviors, but students that embrace failure-yielding behaviors will not tolerate achieving students. Failing students will seek to slow the academic progress of achieving students and will often destroy their opportunity to learn by repeatedly disrupting class. Unfortunately, most schools, parents, and communities do not aggressively confront students who choose failure, even as they deteriorate right before their eyes.

Educators must discover ways to redirect students who use failure-yielding behaviors so that they cannot destroy learning for other students. As advocated by Dr. Bill Macdonald, "attribution retraining" might offer a terrific strategy for American-black students to use for recovery and the attainment of clear learning.

Although the concepts presented have been applied to students, one could extrapolate to apply these same concepts to educators and adults in the families of American-black youngsters. One might imagine the magnitude of the negativism that would occur if those adults engage in disincentive, neglect, model failure-yielding behaviors, or engulf themselves in self-doubt. When adults that are influential in the lives of American-black students embrace the pathology of subordination, engage in bonds of personalism, or stoop to Soul Patrol attitudes, the negativism that impacts American-black children may be irreversible.

## The Threat is Real

American-black adults must face the truth about their children. American-black adults must begin to require American-black students to take personal responsibility for their academic deficiencies. American-black adults must admit that American-black students headed for failure not only pose a detriment to themselves, but they are also a threat to others and society as a whole.

To save these youngsters from failure, poverty, prison, or premature death, internalized self-doubt, institutionalized disincentive, and covenants of neglect must be simultaneously confronted.

# HOW THE LEARNING TRIAD CONTRIBUTES TO THE ACHIEVEMENT GAP

| Learning Triad Members | Institutionalized Disincentive | Covenant of Inaction | Internalized Self-doubt |
|---|---|---|---|
| **Students** | 1. "Crab Mentality" (Live crabs in a bucket pull escaping crabs back)<br><br>2. "Trying to be white" | 1. Sympathize with "bad actors" | 1. "Sour Grapes attitude"<br><br>2. Use what is said as a justification for ineffective effort |
| **Parents/ Community Members** | 1. No role models that look like them in positions of power and influence<br><br>2. "Don't have to live by white folks' rules"<br><br>3. Have no or low accountability standards | 1. No consequences at home for inappropriate school behavior<br><br>2. No consequences at home for inappropriate academic performance | 1. Praise for minimal effort and performance<br><br>2. No motivational dialog at home<br><br>3. Brow beat children<br><br>4. Verbally abuse children |
| **Educators** | 1. Discipline system used is not a compassionate learning tool<br><br>2. Grading and credit system prohibitive | 1. Failure to acknowledge Institutionalized Disincentives<br><br>2. Failure to confront Internalized Self-doubt | 1. Low expectations<br><br>2. Have different consequences for different disaggregated groups |

# SOURCES OF TOXIC POLLUTANTS IN
# THE ACADEMIC ENVIRONMENT

*"Schools where teachers have to deal with such problems as high absenteeism, disrespect and verbal abuse of teachers are usually public schools that have a high population of black students. Students learn more in less disruptive environments. Only in traditional public schools are teachers surrounded by students who get pregnant, treat teachers with contempt, and convey a sense of apathy and indifference to learning. Private schools, even all black private schools do not tolerate such behaviors."*

Abigail and Stephan Thernstrom, *No Excuses*, Closing the Racial Gap in Learning

### The Fight:

During my second week on the job as principal, Marsell Dillon, the assistant principal and security person, Tracey McPike (nicknamed Dick Tracy by the students) explained what was known about the fight that had taken place in science teacher Mr. Carver Albert's class. The fight was between eleventh grade students Mercedes Ford (an A, B student), Lartesha Vaughn (an "Academic Watch" student with low grades and few credits), and Amber Delroy (a strong C, B student).

Security person McPike said, *"According to Mr. Albert, Mercedes was fighting with Lartesha Vaughn, [two American-black female students]. Both were throwing punches, calling each other names, and using profanity. Mr. Albert moved between the two students, separated them, and called for security. After his call, Amber Delroy, [an American-white student] began fussing about the fracas. Amber said that she could not learn with the continuous fracas created by the black students going on in the class. She said, 'My parents pay their tax money for this school and you people make it so that no one can learn.' After that statement, the room erupted into arguments as different students expressed opinions about the remark. Lartesha moved rapidly toward Amber and said, 'Who are you talking about when you said "you people" bitch?' Lartesha then took a swing at Amber and punched her several times while Amber covered her face with her arms."*

Assistant Principal Dillon and I spoke with each student individually; Mercedes, Lartesha, and Amber each told her version of what happened. After I spoke with each girl individually, the mediation session occurred where all three involved girls were in my office together. I explained to the girls the "Rules of Engagement:"

1. Only the adults in the room could ask questions because they were the only ones at the meeting that were not present at the incident and therefore may need further explanation to get a clear understanding of what happened.
2. Each girl would have an opportunity to tell her version of the story.

3. The person speaking could only speak to me and could ask no questions of the other girls.
4. Everyone would be required to listen to the speaker and not interrupt.

I then asked if there was anyone in the room who wanted to be excused from the meeting because she could not agree to these rules. No one declined to stay. I asked the girls which of them wanted to speak first and the mediation session began.

After the mediation session, we asked Mr. Alberts to visit with Assistant Principal Dillon and me in my office. Mr. Alberts was a tall slender man who often talked about his Swedish ancestry. His short blond hair and light blue eyes accentuated his northern European roots. His face was stern and his manner was aloof. The round lenses of his glasses were cradled in thin, wire rims. I asked him what happened concerning the fight that occurred in his classroom.

Mr. Alberts explained, *"The girls were having an argument while I was trying to take attendance."*

Assistant Principal Dillon asked, *"Did you tell them to stop arguing?"*

Mr. Alberts said, *"No; I wanted to get the housekeeping items completed. I intended to ask them right after I finished. I was in a hurry. I didn't have much time remaining to teach the lesson."*

I asked, *"Why did you not have time?"*

Mr. Alberts replied, *"Mrs. Rice [the Spanish teacher] stopped by my room during passing time and she stayed a little longer than I realized. The students had an assignment to complete that was written on the board."*

There was an inadvertent frown on Assistant Principal Dillon's face as she asked, *"Do you think that the fight might have been avoided if you had intervened to stop the arguing?"*

Mr. Alberts said, *"They are always arguing; every day when they come to my class it's an argument."*

*Did you ever report this to the assistant principals?"* I asked.

Mr. Alberts seemed to sense that his actions were not to the liking of we two administrators. He was undaunted as he said, *"No. These kids in this community argue all of the time; it's usually harmless. I find if I ignore it they will eventually quiet down or stop arguing with one person and start with someone else."*

I bit my tongue as Mr. Alberts made those statements. I said, *"Mr. Alberts, I would prefer that you not allow students to disrupt the classroom with arguments; refer them to the assistant principal. They should be in class to learn—not to become the center of attention and overshadow the lesson."*

Mr. Alberts looked at me as if I was pathetically naïve and said, *"You just don't know these kids; when you have been here as long as I have, you will understand— they like to argue and fight. If I got excited every time two of them got into it, all I would be doing all day is stopping arguments. I've got a curriculum to cover Sir."*

The next day the three students and their parents arrived in the office foyer at 8:00 a.m. for the meeting with Assistant Principal Dillon and me. From the beginning, Mercedes' mother, Mrs. Ford, was very supportive. Mrs. Ford was an attractive, slender lady with smooth caramel-colored skin, and large brown eyes. She was dressed in a pinstriped, blue, business suit with a white blouse and blue pumps. She was quick to admonish Mercedes for fighting and concluded that the suspension would be accompanied by extra chores at home. She seemed mainly concerned about two things: that Mercedes received school work so that she could keep up with her classes, and that Mercedes and Lartesha could reconcile or at least form a truce so that there would be no recurrence of fighting.

Lartesha's mother, Ms. Ado, had never been married but she did believe in giving her children their father's last name. She had produced children by three men and Lartesha was the only child in the family that did not have a sibling with the same last name. Ms. Ado was a stout, full-bodied woman, and when she spoke, she seemed angry and on the verge of volatile reaction. Her face was round and fair with large bold features and her three gold teeth were prominent when she was in the middle of conversation. Ms. Ado continuously focused on why Mr. Alberts had not stopped the argument. She contended that there would not have been a fight if "the teacher had done his job." Ms. Ado was convinced that the suspensions should be lifted.

Amber's parents, Mr. And Mrs. Delroy, were dressed neatly, she in a powder blue suit and he in a black suit with a crisp white shirt and bright red tie. Mrs. Delroy, at 50 years old, was short and wide with light brown hair, a pleasant, angular, but serious face, and thin tight lips. Mr. Delroy was a tall, lean, distinguished looking man with steel-blue eyes and close-cut red hair. When they calmly suggested that Lartesha be expelled for her aggression against their daughter, Ms. Ado exploded with anger. The Delroys did not seem affected in the least by Ms. Ado's fury.

Mrs. Ford, Mercedes, Assistant Principal Dillon, and I listened as the Delroys and Ms. Ado squabbled over points of discontent about the incident. I explained that the students would have consequences for their actions and that I would call the parents later that day to state the specifics. I further explained that Amber would receive a consequence but not a suspension because she was not fighting. Upon hearing this, Ms. Ado was livid. She ranted about how Amber was being given special privileges because she was white. I then explained that Amber would receive a consequence for interfering with a teacher's behavioral intervention.

I told Ms. Ado, Lartesha, Mrs. Ford, and Mercedes that fighting would not be tolerated and that they would receive consequences accordingly. Mrs. Ford asked if she could use the phone in the outer foyer to contact her husband to tell him the result. Then she stood and said a cordial goodbye to everyone as she and Mercedes departed. The Delroys stood and expressed their annoyance with the decision by body language more than words, then left, purposely withholding congeniality.

After Amber and her mother and father departed, I explained to Ms. Ado and Lartesha that Lartesha would receive the harshest consequence (a 10-day suspension) because she was the initiator in the fight and she assaulted Amber. Also, Lartesha was not cooperative when the adults intervened. I also decreed that if Lartesha fought at school or at a school event again she would be arrested, suspended for 10 days and I would recommend to the superintendent that she be expelled.

Ms. Ado and Lartesha became extremely volatile and refused to leave. Ms. Ado threatened to involve the NAACP and to hire a lawyer. I was forced to ask Assistant Principal Dillon to call security and have the two of them escorted from the building.

**Academic progress cannot be sustained in schools where the climate and culture permits inappropriate behaviors to flourish.** Educators must publicly denounce such behaviors and courageously counsel students and parents who refuse to comply with the rules and guidelines of the school. **Attention to culture and climate paves the way for academic achievement in schools.**

# TOP FIVE TOXIC POLLUTANTS

Most schools with high numbers of students that have low-test scores, along with an achievement gap, often house educators that have allowed one or more of the typical five academic environment pollutants to flourish, grow, interrupt learning, and proliferate throughout the system:

## 1. Insufficient Effort and Inappropriate Etiquette
Students that demonstrate "insufficient effort" do not exert enough energy toward academic success. Students that display "inappropriate etiquette" have poor manners, do not adhere to protocol, and have distasteful decorum. Sometimes educators notice such behavior more readily when it comes from a student that is struggling academically or is a frequent visitor to the discipline system; but they don't notice it as quickly when

the perpetrator is a student that has strong academic records and rarely has a discipline problem. Nevertheless, educators are consistent when both kinds of students, the challenger and the compliant, receive consequences for inappropriate behavior.

## 2. Distorted Ownership

People who display behaviors that reflect feelings of "distorted-ownership" are usually American-whites. Such feelings are manifested in behaviors that display attitudes that they feel special and want to be given an advantage by institutions and leaders; they display uncompromising behavior; they expect those outside of their group to adhere to harsh policies, while for themselves want softer, more flexible guidelines. Some school leaders and students find the people that suffer from each of these attitudes objectionable and consistently try to avoid them.

American-white parents and students with attitudes of distorted-ownership feel that American-white people, more than others, "own" the district and the specific building within the district where the student attends. People with attitudes of distorted-ownership feel that American-white people are justified in the backlash they display when people outside of their group give input about the operation of the school, or demand to be included in, or have access to what the school has to offer. People with a distorted-ownership attitude feel that American-white people are more entitled than everyone else and are deserving of special privileges because of all that they and others with whom they identify have contributed through the years.

## 3. Inauthentic-Hostility

People that display behaviors that reflect feelings of "Inauthentic-Hostility" are usually American-blacks. Some American-black students have adopted these attitudes because of inequities that they have heard happened to relatives, friends or some other person that is of the same culture or race as they. While many have not personally experienced these inequities, prejudices, hostilities, or degradations themselves, **they are angry on behalf of others and are priming for the perceived "inevitability" that it will happen to them.**

Inauthentic-hostility is also a reaction to perceived distorted-ownership attitudes where American-black parents and students feel that they have license for their alienation because they feel that they have been disregarded, excluded, or unappreciated by the system. **They feel that the system has not been treating them with the same respect and civility as others.** American-black students and parents also feel that American-whites and others in authority are clandestinely trying to keep them from achieving. Parents and students that have feelings of inauthentic-hostility feel that they must claw and scrape for every gain that they make; they feel that the system is controlled by people that have feelings of distorted-ownership and is designed to lock out people like themselves. Inauthentic-hostility is often displayed through false bravado by American-black parents and students because they feel strength in the anger that they cultivate.

## 4. Inert School Leaders

"Inert School Leaders" have **a desperate fear of change, and are secret gatekeepers of the status quo— the way things have always been.** They stall at decision-making concerning racial fairness and desegregation issues; they only capitulate when they absolutely must. Inert school leaders avoid issues of diversity at all costs and overreact if ever confronted with a problem that involves race, ethnicity, or gender. Inert school leaders prefer to bury themselves in efforts to stifle discipline issues, muddle in curriculum, or topics of subject matter staying away from ideas that bridge gaps and embrace cooperation and collaboration between people. Inert school leaders seem most concerned with the protection of their jobs, their own position, status, and acquisition of status. Although they may know the appropriate rhetoric and may speak it well, the academic achievement of students and service to families is at best only secondary to them.

### 5. Counter-productive parents

"Counter-productive parents" **adopt the behaviors of bullies.** When bullying parents visit schools they are often combative, aggressive, threatening, abrasive and abusive to school personnel. Counter-productive parents also assume the behavior of being "ghosts." They are difficult to contact (wrong phone numbers and addresses, or no phone numbers, and offer no emergency contact person), rarely return phone calls, or answer notes or letters, and they only visit schools when they go to defend the inappropriate behaviors of their children.

Counter-productive parents are extremely difficult for school staff members to approach because they seem perpetually angry at the school district and the educators attempting to help their children learn. **They insistently blame others for problems that have been created by themselves and their child.** Counter-productive parents regularly support their children when their children are wrong and enable their children who often have rebellious behavior and attitudes. These parents also tend to be manipulative, self-involved, and non-directive.

## THE THREE FACES OF AMERICAN-WHITE TEACHERS

Another situation that might become an issue among American-black students is how teachers react to them. American-blacks experiencing American-white teachers soon discover that the American-white teachers have at least one of three faces: the xenophobic teacher, the paternalistic teacher, or the purpose-driven teacher. To complicate matters, sometimes American-white teachers blend one or more of these attitudes and psychologies into their interactions with American-blacks. The complexity of this situation is further exacerbated when white teachers move in and out of each of these faces within days, hours, minutes, or even seconds. Many white teachers do not recognize that they embrace these faces; others do, but do not regularly or openly admit to this.

**Xenophobic American-white teachers are often chauvinistic and prejudiced toward American-black students, parents and colleagues.** Xenophobic American-white teachers are regularly intolerant and narrow-minded in dealings with American-blacks. At their worst, xenophobic American-white teachers are bigoted and racist in their interactions with American-blacks. They regularly avoid being confronted about this because they know that American-blacks that embrace mainstream and green-culture attitudes do not like to be accused of playing the race card and other blacks use the race card with such regularity that it often falls on deaf ears. They also realize that other whites are reluctant to challenge them. Consequently, xenophobic whites have some insulation from criticism.

**Paternalistic American-white teachers most often are condescending and patronizing to American-black students, parents and colleagues.** Paternalistic American-whites are sometimes pompous, sometimes haughty, but always assume an air of superiority. Paternalistic American-white teachers are protagonists for systems where minimal needs and services are supplied to American-blacks in order to keep American-blacks dependent on the provider.

**Purpose-driven American-white teachers are direct in their efforts to pursue the idea of educating students without a predisposition about the student's race, color, or gender.** Purpose-driven American-white teachers have high expectations and are determined to be principled when interacting with any and all students. Teachers driven by purpose are motivated by reason, goals, objectives, and persistent resolve to impart knowledge to students.

American-blacks probably have the most difficulty interacting with xenophobic and paternalistic American-white teachers. Such teachers are often successful at smothering the possibilities of American-black students and they are often able to do this without reproach because blacks that challenge them are most often accused of "playing the race card" or simply whining. Also, American-whites are slow to recognize other American-whites that are xenophobic and paternalistic. Even when American-whites recognize xenophobic and paternalistic American-whites they are reluctant to "blow the whistle." The exposure of xenophobic and paternalistic American-whites by other American-whites is not something that has been openly supported or encouraged by the wider community of whites.

American-blacks experience academic success on a regular basis when interacting with purpose-driven American-white teachers rather than the xenophobic and paternalistic ones. Such teachers recognize the uniqueness of the culture of American-blacks without minimizing or diminishing their existence and Americanism. Purpose-driven American-white teachers exude caring and high expectations and do not compromise this attitude for American-black students. Purpose-driven teachers are equitable in their relationships with students, parents, and colleagues regardless of race, religion, gender, or sexual orientation.

Unfortunately xenophobic and paternalistic American-white teachers together with American-blacks that choose failure regularly criticize and demonize purpose-driven teachers. Both groups reject purpose-driven American-white teachers, but for different reasons; the former because purpose-driven teachers cause the deficiencies of xenophobic and paternalistic American-white teachers to be illuminated in a negative light and the latter because purpose-driven teachers require students to be accountable. Further, when students are required to be accountable, teachers are required to be accountable as well.

In the minds of many American-blacks, xenophobic and paternalistic American-whites have been clandestinely and consistently supported by American society in general and American-whites in particular. Many American-blacks feel that xenophobic and paternalistic whites have worked in the past and continue to work to hold blacks back and devise and support the subordination of blacks.

Sometimes American-blacks become extremely upset over this and have negative emotional reactions to xenophobic and paternalistic behaviors. Sensitive educators understand that American-blacks involved in the Learning Triad (students, educators, parents) often must face the three faces of American-white educators. Whether educators, parents, or students many American-blacks within the Learning Triad are confronted with the realities of having to negotiate the attitudes and psychology of American-white educators.

# THE THREE FACES OF AMERICAN-BLACK TEACHERS

American-blacks experiencing American-black educators soon discover that black educators have at least one of three faces, too: the black-nationalist educator, the molly-coddler educator, or the purpose-driven educator. To complicate matters, sometimes American-black educators blend one or more of these attitudes and psychologies in their interactions with American-black students and their parents. As with the three faces of American-white educators, the complexity of this situation further proliferates when black educators move in and out of each of these faces within days, hours, minutes, or even seconds. Many black educators do not recognize that they embrace these faces; others do, but do not regularly or openly admit to this.

**Black-nationalist American-black educators are often autonomous separatists that view black people as victims of white imperialistic racism and promote arrogance as an appropriate disposition to present to white authority figures.** They put forth the attitude that black people are the injured party and have been duped, fooled, and tricked into a psychology of subordination. Black- nationalists put forward the idea that black people should not view themselves as American; that they are victims and should be angry at white people. They further suggest that black people are different and should not have to obey white folks' rules. Black-nationalistic American-black educators are regularly intolerant and narrow-minded. At their worst, black-nationalistic American-black educators present an exterior that is often viewed as bigoted and prejudiced against whites and the American system.

**Molly-coddler American-black educators most often are overprotective with American-black students, parents and colleagues.** Molly-coddler American-black educators regularly spoil and pamper American-black students—requiring minimal effort or quality from American-black students, their parents, and American-black educator colleagues. Molly-coddler American-black educators are often seen as babying, pandering, and indulgent toward American-black students. In this psychology, molly-coddlers put forward the idea that America has an obligation to give to American-blacks but no authority to demand anything of them. Molly-coddlers advocate that American-blacks should not be held to the same requirements as whites because the system is unfair, racially biased, and was created to suppress blacks. The molly-coddlers also present the idea that the mothers of American-black students can exercise control over schools, and therefore they can get away with stuff.

**Purpose-driven American-black educators are direct in their efforts to pursue the idea of educating students without predisposition to the student's race, color, or gender.** Purpose-driven American-black educators are determined to be principled when interacting with any and all students. Educators driven by purpose are motivated by reason, goals, objectives, and persistent resolve to impart knowledge to students.

American-blacks probably have the most difficulty interacting with black-nationalistic and molly- coddler American-black educators. Such teachers are often successful at smothering the possibilities of American-black students and they are often able to do this without reproach because blacks that challenge them are most often accused by other American-blacks of being "oreos" (white on the inside but black on the outside), Uncle Toms (doing whatever pleases whites), or simply "trying to be white."

Students that embrace the attitudes of the black-nationalist and the molly coddlers commonly believe that traditional education is a white thing and not important to black people because street knowledge and Afro-centric knowledge is more useful. The students often view being a thug as being more appealing than being a responsible citizen. The students influenced by black-nationalists and molly coddlers are convinced that knowledge about black people and their culture is more important than knowledge about the world of ideas beyond them.

Also, American-blacks are slow to disapprove of other American-blacks that are black-nationalists and molly-coddlers. Even when American-blacks disapprove of American-black educators that are black-nationalist and molly-coddlers they are reluctant to criticize them. The open condemnation of American-blacks that are black-nationalist and molly-coddlers by other American-blacks is not something that has been supported or encouraged by the wider community of blacks.

American-black students usually experience more academic success when interacting with purpose-driven American-black educators than when interacting with the black-nationalistic and molly coddler ones. Such educators recognize the uniqueness of the culture of American-blacks without glamorizing or exalting black people. Purpose-driven American-black educators exude caring and high expectations and are equitable in their relationships with students, parents, and colleagues regardless of race, religion, gender, or sexual orientation.

Many American-black educators that are black-nationalists and molly-coddlers regularly criticize and demonize purpose-driven educators. Both groups reject purpose-driven American-black educators because purpose-driven educators require students to be accountable and demonstrate that the students can prosper and succeed in spite of obstacles.

**In the minds of many misguided American-blacks, black-nationalists and molly-coddlers are the real spokespersons of the American-black community.** It is believed by some that such voices speak the actual truth about the condition and attitudes of American-black people. In the minds of many American-blacks people that sympathize with black-nationalistic and molly-coddler attitudes believe that black-nationalists and molly-coddlers are the authentic warriors and nurturers of the American-black community.

## Things Are Not Always As They Appear

It is important that Americans that support and believe in efforts to bring quality to public education and to the academic condition of American-black students realize and recognize from where opposition comes. Those who advocate for quality in education and seek the academic uplift of American-black students would be wise to remember that every person that seemingly endeavors to protect and defend American-black children is not necessarily a friend to American-black children. Likewise, everyone that is seemingly strict and insistent upon academic rigor from American-black students is not necessarily a foe to American-black children.

# ADDRESSING THE ACHIEVEMENT GAP

The achievement gap can be eradicated with deliberate speed when educators embrace social justice, by modeling honest impartial fairness and integrity that is publicly shared within the school; and developing and maintaining a climate of inclusion where students enjoy an all-embracing, all-inclusive, all-encompassing environment. Parents and community members can help eliminate the gap by advocating compassionate diligence within society where people are encouraged to be thorough, meticulous, conscientious, and attentive in efforts to show benevolence, consideration, kindheartedness, empathy, and caring toward each other.

> **The achievement gap cannot stand where academic equity exists; the two cannot coexist.**

Members of the community can motivate American-black students by making opportunities available, chances and prospects accessible, obtainable, and offered to all qualified people regardless of race, gender, or religious preference. American-black students can better prepare themselves by embracing self determination in strength of mind, willpower, purpose, and fortitude. They can also attain necessary qualifications and seek to gain, obtain, and acquire training, education and credentials. The achievement gap cannot stand where academic equity exists; the two cannot coexist.

Those within the Learning Triad (parents, educators, and students) can utilize the strategies of Academic Equity to eradicate the achievement gap. Adults in schools and communities can confront institutionalized disincentive with perpetual encouragement. When the covenant of neglect is met with deliberate nurturing, internalized self-doubt will be eliminated by infusing children with pervasive confidence. Adults must use strategies of focused diligence, quiet determination, and persistent perseverance to engage the negative mind-sets of destructive collusion, wasted opportunities, and defeatist attitudes.

## RESPONSE TO THE ACHIEVEMENT GAP

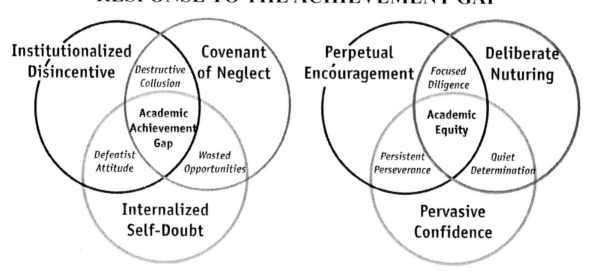

**The Antidote for the Achievement Gap: When the Academic Equity Venn is superimposed onto the Achievement Gap Venn, answers to the puzzle of low achievement of American-black students are apparent. The only question remaining is whether those within the Learning Triad are willing to follow the plan.**

While following the QUO Process, those within the Learning Triad can utilize strategies to gain academic equity to eradicate the achievement gap.

## Address Institutionalized Disincentive with Personal Encouragement

To confront institutionalized disincentive, parents and community members, students, and educators must be committed to uninterrupted, unending, and eternal inspiration and cheering for the success of students. Those in the Learning Triad must agree to require from each other the continuous encouragement of students. Institutionalized disincentive cannot stand where personal encouragement is purposefully done and initiatives are put in place to help students be successful; the two cannot coexist. When the adults in the lives of students are committed to personally engage students the students will demonstrate focused diligence where they will stay attentive, alert, and involved with academic achievement.

## Engage Self-Doubt with Pervasive Confidence

Pervasive confidence is all-encompassing. It envelops students and helps them become persistent in their efforts toward academic success. When students are taught to believe that they can accomplish a task no matter how unachievable it may at first seem, nothing can hold them back. Adults that perpetually encourage students to embrace a pervasive confidence draw a sense of persistent perseverance from the students. When students are taught to persevere, it is rare that feelings of defeat will dominate their attitudes. After learning the art of "little chunks," students become proficient at breaking down big projects into smaller pieces and they can complete one little chunk at a time. Before they know it, the whole job is finished and students realize it wasn't so difficult after all. **Success breeds confidence and the darkness of self-doubt cannot endure in the luminosity of pervasive confidence.**

## The Antidote for the Covenant of Neglect is Deliberate Nurturing

Educators and adult family members of students can enrich, care for, and help develop young people. The adults must be deliberate, premeditated, and intentional in their nurturing of students. Covenants of neglect cannot survive when persistent and deliberate nurturing occurs. When the adults in the lives of students deliberately nurture the students and encourage the students to project pervasive confidence, the students will emit a quiet determination. Students that are relentless in efforts toward success learn not to waste opportunities.

## Progressive Coalition Rejects the Pathology of Subordination

Plenty of Americans—black and white, student and adult, educators and parents, and politicians and business leaders—reject the pathology of subordination. This progressive coalition aspires to meet, help, or celebrate American-black students and help elevate American-black people that meet or exceed accountability standards, requirements, and achieve credentials necessary to validate and qualify themselves in the mainstream culture of success in America.

# Part Two
# The Government's Response to the Wake-Up Call

# Chapter 3
# Understanding the Spirit of "No Child Left Behind"

*"The achievement gap is worse today than it was fifteen years ago; in the 1970s and 1980s, it was closing but around 1988 it began to widen with no turn around in sight. No Child Left Behind legislation is attempting to close the achievement gap. Because of NCLB, affluent districts will no longer be able to coast along hiding their low-performing black students in overall averages that make their schools look good."*

Abigail and Stephan Thernstrom, *No Excuses: Closing the Racial Gap in Learning*

**Martha's Misgivings:**

The teacher's union called a special Faculty Advisory Council meeting with the superintendent to express concerns about the initiatives that I, as high school principal, advocated. The meeting had not gone as the union expected. The superintendent and the assistant superintendent explained that the district hired me to bring change and that test scores must improve. They explained that the Board of Education emphatically demanded change at the high school.

The two of them explained that if the high school did not make the changes necessary to move the school toward adequate yearly progress (AYP) and meet the No Child Left Behind (NCLB) deadlines, then severe government imposed consequences could occur. The state might privatize the school and everyone might lose their jobs. They explained the inevitability of accepting change for the better and that the faster the high school teachers worked as a team with the principal, the more quickly positive change and improvement would occur.

The superintendent spoke to a quiet room. For the first time, many of the teachers realized the gravity of the situation. The superintendent had previously used the "soft sell" approach: listening to staff members talk about what wonderful teachers taught at the high school; how well they worked together; and how the students would do so much better if their home lives improved and had more attentive parents. But this time, the superintendent intensely conveyed a sense of looming urgency.

He politely "laid it on the line" in a matter-of-fact, straightforward way. No one could misunderstand him. After the superintendent finished his remarks, the staff sat in silence for a few moments, then continued with the meeting. I never before witnessed a superintendent so forthright with a faculty.

After the meeting concluded, Martha, a veteran special education teacher, beckoned for me to approach her. Her thin lips drew tight against her teeth when she smiled. Enough time elapsed since the end of the teacher's meeting that most of the smaller impromptu meetings were slowly winding down. Many teachers asked me clarifying questions as I walked from the library toward my office. Some pulled me aside to pledge support for the Quo Process initiatives. Martha wanted further explanation about something discussed at the meeting.

*"Dylan Tyler, after the meeting, was talking to some of us,"* she said.
I knew Dylan well. He played a major role in the teacher's union.

*"Yeah, what did he say?"* I asked.

*"He said that No Child Left Behind legislation is an insidious Republican plot to privatize all of the schools in America,"* she began talking in low tones.

*"Do you believe that?"* I asked.

*"I don't know what to believe."* Martha, as she leaned against the wall said, *"I know that people probably think that the teachers here are terrible because the students are doing poorly on the state and national standardized tests."*

She shifted to stand straight, and as she spoke she stared into my eyes. *"We have some darned good teachers here and it is too bad that this NCLB stuff is making us look bad. Some of these kids have no home life, no direction, no positive role models, and no motivation from their parents to do well in school. The teachers are doing the best that we can with what we have to work with."*

I looked away for a moment then made eye contact again and asked, *"Let's say that all that you have said is true. We still must ask ourselves, what more we can do to help the students reach the benchmarks? If they do not reach the standards whether NCLB exists or not, they will continue to fall further behind the competition they must face as they move beyond high school. How will they survive? What will be their quality of life? How will they be able to care for themselves and their families? If they become part of a hopeless underclass how will they respond? If we don't help them meet the expectations that everyone else is expected to meet, what will happen to them?"*

Martha was quiet for a moment as she obviously struggled with what I said. *"Do you think he's right?"* she asked.

*"Who?"* I asked.

*"Mr. Tyler,"* she said.

*"Who knows, and I don't think it matters,"* I said. *"The fact remains that American-black students suffer academically and teachers have the power to help. NCLB points that out and some people blame the messenger on this. Anyone with a conscience that comes to understand the facts behind this realizes something must be done to improve this situation and advocate urgent change."*

Martha smiled at me and reassured me that she supported me in the change process. As she walked away another teacher moved toward me and accompanied me to my office. It seemed that all of a sudden everyone wanted to talk to me. Just that morning the very ones who now wanted to talk had groused that I seemed unapproachable.

## The Road to NCLB

The road begins in 1954, when the Brown vs. Topeka Supreme Court case ruled that schools must be desegregated at all deliberate speed.

In 1964, Title IV of the Civil Rights Act of 1964 called for a survey "concerning the lack of availability of equal educational opportunity by reason of race, color, religion, or national origin in pubic educational institutions at all levels." James S. Coleman, then a professor in the department of social relations at Johns Hopkins University and Ernest Q. Campbell of Vanderbilt University, performed the landmark 1966 study, "Equality of Educational Opportunity," which became instrumental in promoting racial balance between schools.

Coleman studied 600,000 children at 4,000 schools and found that most children attended schools where they were the majority race. Further, schooling between American-white and minority schools was similar. Teachers' training, teachers' salaries, and curriculum were relatively equal. The results, however, found that minority children were a few years behind that of the American-whites and that the gap widened by the high school years. In conclusion, the academic achievement was related to family background in the early years, but going to school allowed for a greater disparity between the academic differences between American-whites and American-blacks.

Coleman presented a report to the U.S. Congress concluding that poor American-black children did better academically in integrated, middle-class schools. Coleman's work had a far-reaching impact on government education policy.

The following year, another study conducted by the Civil Rights Commission, "Racial Isolation in the Public Schools" confirmed Coleman's findings. The government introduced a policy of Affirmative Action to racially integrate schools and to end de facto segregation produced by income level and neighborhood ethnic composition. A result of the policy was the busing of school children to schools outside their neighborhoods. The aim was to achieve racial balance between schools by preventing American-black enrollment from exceeding 60 percent.

# A NATION AT RISK

The education agenda of the first Bush Sr. Administration was basically that of the Reagan administration, which had issued a report called "A Nation at Risk" in 1983. According to that report, the educational establishment was heading in the wrong direction. The educational dimensions of the risk have been documented in testimony received by the commission. Some of the findings were:

- International comparisons of student achievement have revealed that on 19 academic tests American students were never first or second and, in comparison with other industrialized nations, were last seven times.
- Some 23 million American adults are functionally illiterate by the simplest tests of everyday reading, writing, and comprehension.
- About 13 percent of all 17-year-olds in the United States can be considered functionally illiterate. Functional illiteracy among minority youth may run as high as 40 percent.
- Average achievement of high school students on most standardized tests is now lower than when Sputnik was launched in the 1950s.
- Over half the population of gifted students do not match their tested ability with comparable achievement in school.
- The College Board's Scholastic Aptitude Tests (SAT) demonstrate a virtually unbroken decline from 1963 to 1980. Average verbal scores fell over 50 points and average mathematics scores dropped nearly 40 points.
- College Board achievement tests also reveal consistent declines in recent years in such subjects as physics and English.
- Both the number and proportion of students demonstrating superior achievement on the SATs (i.e., those with scores of 650 or higher) have also dramatically declined.
- Many 17-year-olds do not possess the "higher order" intellectual skills we should expect of them. Nearly 40 percent cannot draw inferences from written material; only one-fifth can write a persuasive essay; and only one-third can solve a mathematics problem requiring several steps.
- There was a steady decline in science achievement scores of U.S. 17-year-olds as measured by national assessments of science in 1969, 1973, and 1977.
- Between 1975 and 1980, remedial mathematics courses in public four-year colleges increased by 72 percent and now constitute one-quarter of all mathematics courses taught in those institutions.
- Average tested achievement of students graduating from college is also lower.
- Business and military leaders complain that they are required to spend millions of dollars on costly remedial education and training programs in such basic skills

as reading, writing, spelling, and computation. The Department of the Navy, for example, reported to the commission that one-quarter of its recent recruits cannot read at the ninth grade level, the minimum needed simply to understand written safety instructions. Without remedial work they cannot even begin, much less complete, the sophisticated training essential in much of the modern military.

It is also important to note that one portion of the 1966 Coleman report explained differences in academic achievement between American-whites and American-blacks as a byproduct of a culture of poverty. This culture of poverty supposedly had a greater influence on American-blacks because of a higher concentration of poverty among American-blacks. Because of the information about the culture of poverty, the 1966 Coleman report was cited by school districts around the country as evidence that integrating American-black students into schools with predominantly American-white student populations would have little or no effect on student achievement. Many of the same school districts used one piece of information in the Nation at Risk report to show that the attention given to minority students had a negative effect on the academic achievement of accelerated, talented, and gifted American-white students.

## THE 1990 SANDIA REPORT

The important question became: What actually happened after most of the racially segregated school systems were desegregated and after people received information from the Nation at Risk report? The Sandia Report was commissioned by the Bush, Sr. administration to review data collected by the National Center for Education Statistics of the United States Department of Education through a testing program called the National Assessment of Educational Progress.

According to the 1990 Sandia Report, the test score gap between whites and blacks declined during the 1970s and 1980s. Even as the income gap between American-blacks and American-whites was widening during the 1980s, the test score gap was decreasing (Berliner and Biddle, 1995, *The Manufactured Crisis,* page 26).

**The Sandia Report didn't agree with the "Nation at Risk" rhetoric about a rising tide of mediocrity eroding the foundations of America's educational system.** It seemed that the educational establishment's quest to obtain more equal outcomes between students was harming the best and the brightest students, or so the argument goes. The problem with the Sandia report was it found that high-achieving students made significant gains during an era of "forced bussing," widespread resistance to, and rejection of ability-grouping, and the diversion of resources to poor people, the disabled, and other "special interest groups."

Regardless of how the information was and is used by different "special interest groups" the fact remains that the standardized test scores of most of America's school children are not where most adults think that they ought to be and that the scores of American-black students were low before forced or voluntary bussing and are now low again. Something has to be done to bring the scores of all the students up and it has been well documented that when strategies are implemented to help raise the scores of American-black students, the scores of American-white students go up as well.

# NCLB AIMS TO CLOSE THE ACHIEVEMENT GAP IN EDUCATION

The public education system must connect students to the world of academic accomplishment—putting them on the ladder of economic opportunity, while introducing them to the history, culture, and institutions of America. No Child Left Behind intends to make certain that schools make these opportunities available to all students, including American-black students, students from low-resource families, and students with special situations.

In efforts to uplift students and upgrade the quality of education, President George W. Bush signed NCLB into law on January 8, 2002. It was to provide nearly $1 billion a year over five years to strengthen public schools. The No Child Left Behind (NCLB) Act affects almost every public school and district in America. **The act's overall purpose is to ensure that children in every classroom enjoy the benefits of well-prepared teachers, research-based curriculum and safe learning environments.** NCLB is a blend of new requirements, new incentives and new resources. Some of its provisions will challenge states, schools, and districts to take immediate action. Others will be implemented over the long term. NCLB is an opportunity to align federal and state initiatives in common support of higher student achievement, stronger public schools and a better-prepared teacher workforce.

**NCLB legislation aims for universal proficiency** by insisting that public schools implement plans, activities, and programs that will uplift American-black students, students from low-resource families, and students with special situations. NCLB legislation requires that schools show adequate yearly progress with student test scores and demands that states create standardized mandatory tests that create accountability for the schools. If improvement cannot be shown, or at least progress made, the NCLB legislation mandates consequences for non-compliant schools.

**NCLB legislation endeavors to persuade educators to implement strategies that will close the achievement gap.** Because of NCLB, affluent districts will no longer coast along, allowing their low-performing American-black students to be concealed, wallowing in obscurity within overall high averages. Under NCLB as measured by standardized tests, schools must account for all students and in particular report scores for those from the most challenging situations. But American-black students must also do their part. American-black students must come to school on time, attend every class, listen with their full attention, and "burn the midnight oil."

## Is it a Perfect Solution?

Is NCLB too idealistic in that the designers think that 100 percent of the students will be able to reach the benchmark by 2014, or at any time for that matter? Maybe, but it's a great target and it's better than having no target as was the case before NCLB. Would it be nice to have more money to better finance the NCLB guidelines and initiatives? Yes, but it would be nice to have more money for any worthwhile endeavor upon which people decide to embark; but there are many advancements toward NCLB expectations that can be accomplished without new money by reorganizing for better efficiency the way existing finances are spent.

Is NCLB ambitious in its design and vision? Yes, and this is a good thing because America needs to be ambitious and visionary when it comes to the future of the children and American posterity.

When discussing the NCLB legislation, many people stress about the accountability measures and the attempts to create viable consequences. What might be more productive is a concentration on the main point and spirit of the legislation; to nurture the achieving students while uplifting low achieving students. **The NCLB legislation has basically four components: uplift, progress, accountability, and consequences (UPAC).** Accountability and consequences support uplift and progress, the main goals of NCLB.

## Putting Teeth in the NCLB

To make certain that American-black students, students from low-resource families, and students with special situations have a chance for success in mainstream American society, NCLB legislation added accountability measures to encourage educators in individual schools to academically engage and motivate students to achieve. NCLB expects states to set standards and require standardized testing in all public schools to determine if students perform at appropriate levels. Thus far, the tests have revealed the fact that American-blacks learn less than they should or could.

Some educators, parents, and students attacked the standardized tests and denied the tests' validity. However, in September 2000, the research organization, Public Agenda, found that only 11 percent of parents think that American leaders place too much value on standardized tests. Seventy-one percent of parents supported testing students at a young age so that teachers can identify those who need help. Fifty-five percent of parents believe nothing is wrong with teaching to the test. Seventy-eight percent of parents of American-black students agreed that testing calls attention to a problem that needs solving. Furthermore, 65 percent of parents and 70 percent of the general public believe that students should pass a statewide test before they graduate from high school. The percentages went up when people discovered that students could take the test several times.

Finally, to put teeth into the program, NCLB legislation added consequences for inadequate progress on standardized tests. The federal law says that the Department of Education will withhold federal funds from schools that use title funding but do not meet standards. Parents have the right to transfer their children from failing schools to other schools within the district. District schools that do meet standards must accept students from a failing school in the same district. More advocates for vouchers have surfaced, too.

## Internal and External Review

To be sure educators in schools are meeting the requirements of NCLB many states have implemented school improvement processes that educators in individual schools and school districts must fulfill. The general way states organize this is to insist that educators within schools and districts scrutinize the overall operation of their schools with an internal review.

The internal review has several components designed to help educators take a critical look at their schools and school districts. After the internal review educators in schools and school districts are expected by state officials to make positive change. To discover if students are prospering academically because of what occurs at school, state officials provide standardized tests that are administered yearly at targeted grade levels. A state average of percentage of students reaching the benchmark at each level of the tests is measured and educators at every school may compare the percentages of students that reached the benchmark at each level within individual schools to the state percentages.

State officials may also send teams of experts to schools throughout the state at predetermined intervals to conduct external reviews of the organization and inner workings of individual schools and school districts.

## Call to Action

In effect, the Coleman, Nation at Risk, and Sandia reports were messages of warning to the American people that public education needs attention. NCLB and State School Improvement initiatives are reactions to the warnings. Self-starting educators across America are preemptively addressing situations in their own individual schools that will help students improve academically and to reorganize the overall operation of schools to perform with greater effectiveness.

# Part Three
# QUO Process: A
# Definitive Solution

# Chapter 4
# A Problem of Focus

*"In the Chinese language, two characters represent the word "learning." The character means "to study." It is composed of two parts: a symbol that means "to accumulate knowledge" is placed above a symbol for a child in a doorway. The second character means "to practice constantly," and it shows a bird developing the ability to leave the nest. The upper symbol represents flying; the lower symbol youth. For the Asian mind, learning is ongoing. "Study" and "practice constantly," together, suggest that learning should mean: "mastery of the way of self-improvement."*

Peter Senge, *A Fifth Discipline Resource: Schools That Learn*

### The Rap Life:

He was small for a ninth grader, more the size of a seventh grader, probably 115 pounds, slender and about 5'3" tall. His face was thin and his jaw was long with high cheek bones. His dark-hued skin helped accent his perpetually flashing smile. Life amused him. We looked at each other across the table in my office.

*"I thought my mama was going to be here,"* he said.

*"She should be here any minute,"* I said.

Almost as soon as I spoke my secretary appeared at my door to announce that Mrs. Jordan had arrived. Mrs. Jordan said hello to her son and he smiled and returned the hello. I explained that we met to talk about Dash's grades. He received five "F's" on his last report card and for the second time, his name appeared on the academic watch list. Mrs. Jordan looked at Dash and told him to sit up straight and stop grinning.

*"Look at him. Daeshon does not live in reality,"* she said. *"I have to put up with this at home every day."*

I asked Dash why he continuously received F's on his report cards. He smiled and leaned forward on the table.

*"I'm going to be a rap star and you don't need a high school diploma for that,"* he said.

*"See what I mean?"* his mother said. *"The boy has no sense of the real world. This is what he tells me every day. You see what I have to put up with? He thinks that he is going to be the next Sloopy Log..."*

*"Snoop Dawg,"* Dash smiled as he corrected her.

*"Daeshon..."* I began.

*"You can call me Dash,"* he said.

*"Dash? Where did that come from?"* Mrs. Jordan said.

*"That's gonna be my label name when I make my albums, Dash said."*

*"Dash or Daeshon, why do you even show up to school every day?"* I continued with my question.

*"Because my mama makes me,"* Dash smiled his crooked smile as he spoke.

*"Now what do you do about something like that?"* Mrs. Jordan said. *"This is what I put up with every day. The boy does not understand. I think that you can see the problem."*

*"Daeshon, what can I do to help you get those grades up?"* I asked.

*"Nothing, I don't care if they come up. I don't worry about grades anyway. You ever seen the T.V. show Cribs?"*

I shook my head, no.

*"It shows what kind of houses and cars rap singers have. They have big houses, really nice cars. Many have three and more cars, really expensive cars. A lot of the rappers don't have high school diplomas. So that's what I'm going to be."*

*"Now Daeshon, honey, you cannot be sure that you will be a rap star so why don't you try hard in school and get your education?"* his mother said.

Again the freshman smiled at his mother.

*"Don't worry Mama, after I release my first album it will be number one and I
will buy you a new crib, a car and you will not have to work another day in your
life."*

I could see that Dash frustrated Mrs. Jordan. A single mother with an only child,
she wanted the best for him but she felt that she could not crack the delusional
shell that he had created for himself. Her eyes silently pleaded to me for help.

I looked directly at Daeshon as I spoke, *"Daeshon, I want you to hear me plain;
I care about you and want you to be successful. If you are going to be a Rapper I
want you to be the best Rapper in the world, therefore I am going to have to help
you get ready."*

Daeshon sat up in his chair with a confused look on his face. Mrs. Jordan looked
at me as if I had failed to get her message.

I continued, *"I expect you to make B's or better from now on in your English
classes because Rappers have to be good with the use of language. I want to see
your name in every writing contest that you can get into. If you want to be good
at something you have got to work at it."*

I could sense that Mrs. Jordan was beginning to see were I was going with my
comments. The smile had left Daeshon's face.

I said, *"I expect you to get B's or better in math classes because since you are going
to be making so much money you are going to have to understand mathematics. I
expect you to make B's or better in social studies because you are going to have
to understand how to deal with people. You will probably have agents, producers,
partners, and an entourage and hangers on, and you need to make at least B's or
better in science because you need a full understanding of the scientific method
so that you can work through problems that will surely occur in your business
endeavors."*

Daeshon looked as if he had seen a ghost as he said, *"But the Rappers out there
now didn't finish high school and they are doing alright."* I said, *"I do not want
you to just be alright, I want you to be the best Rapper Daeshon. I'll bet that you
will find that the best Rappers would encourage you to graduate if you could talk
to them."*

Daeshon seemed to be thinking hard about what I said. I then said, *"I have got
to be tough on you Dash...to get you ready, so I'm grounding you here at school.
Until those grades come up you cannot travel on field trips, go to all school
assemblies, attend extracurricular activities; no football games, no basketball
games, no dances."* Daeshon looked up and from me to his mother pleading as he
said, *"But I already have my ticket to the Homecoming Dance and I got a date*

*with Latesha Howard."* I conjured the most pitiful look that I could and said, *"We can reimburse you money for the ticket."*

Suddenly, life wasn't so amusing to Daeshon anymore. I could see Mrs. Jordan try to conceal a smile as she shifted in her seat, placed her hand over her mouth and cleared her throat.

Data shows that students who demonstrate academic poor performance face a bleak future. The bottom line is: American-black students must accept that education is their passport to success. American-black students, as do all students, need to understand that in order to be successful in the green culture, the ideas and concepts of the green culture must be embraced, such as: respect for authority, the rights and property of others, justice and fair play, obeying the rules, and life and human dignity.

*"Education is the key civil rights and economic issue of our time. There is nothing more important to the long-term growth of our economy and to the success of our democracy and society than making sure that the United States has a highly skilled, well-educated workforce."*

Eli Broad, Founder, The Broad Foundation

This is a problem of focus. This is the problem to solve and **this is the time for an expansion in the fight for civil rights to include the struggle toward academic equity**. American-black adult family members of American-black children could take the lead in this struggle—and it is a struggle, because American-black children must hurry to catch-up. Educators also have much of the responsibility in this effort because it is our profession, our skill, and our expertise that can catapult the American-black students into equity.

> **Educators are in a struggle against ignorance**

Educators are in a struggle against ignorance and collectively we have not addressed this situation with enough determination and urgency. Leaders with the best plans who successfully communicate those plans to their colleagues and other stakeholders most often experience the greatest success of implementation. Educators must learn from this reality and understand that we must create a plan for each district and each individual school that is successfully communicated to colleagues and other stakeholders so that ignorance can be defeated.

Educators have a difficult task that could be softened by the concept of "attribution retraining" explained in the opening quote of Chapter 2. **Attribution retraining could be expanded to relate to raising the consciousness level of students concerning possibilities that wait for those with a good education.**

Strong educators could lead American-black students toward greater possibilities in their lives by encouraging them to respond to academic rigor by retracing their steps to find mistakes or figuring out alternative ways of approaching a problem instead of giving up. Educators who care can help American-black students understand that attributing their failures to insufficient effort, lack of information, or reliance on ineffective strategies rather than to lack of ability makes it less difficult to move toward recovery and success in the mainstream green culture.

## Expectations Play a Key Role

Most often children will try to do what adults expect of them. The adults in families and educators have an opportunity to take hold of the situation and form coalitions to help students get better. When adults in families and educators present the same message of high expectations to students, the students will respond more positively, completely, and at a faster rate than most people might imagine.

## At Home With High Performance

The Home Observation for Measurement of the Environment (HOME) scale suggests a number of home factors affecting school performance:

- The number of age-appropriate books in the home
- The frequency of parent involvement with their children's home work
- The number of educational trips on which parents take their youngsters
- The amount of quality time by parents spent with youngsters
- The parent's emotional support and physical expressions of affection toward the child
- The parent's patient attention to the child's questions
- The type of discipline other than physical punishment that parents use

If American-black children are to be saved it will be partially because of a commitment by American-black adults. If it takes tough love to get it accomplished, then tough love there should be. American-black adults must insist that the American-black youngsters do as well or better academically as any other group of American young people regardless of the obstacles.

# UNINTENTIONAL CONSEQUENCES OF ACCOUNTABILITY REGARDING ATTENDANCE

Traditionally, when educators have discussed the discipline issues of education, the standard channel of thought has been that it is of tremendous importance to find ways to get students to stay in school and to keep those that want to drop out from dropping out. Those that seek to discover ways to hold educators accountable often use those two determinates as part of the litmus tests for that accountability. As a result, several unintentional consequences have occurred because of the pursuit of those ends.

Now, the message has been sent that educators are expected to be "creative" in trying to keep youngsters in and entice them to return to school even when they are resistant. Educators are expected to "beat the bushes" to lure drop outs back to schools. Some of the schools give prizes, special privileges, and even money to students to get them to return to school. Unfortunately, in far too many cases, students that are coaxed back to school are either wrecking havoc in the halls, cafeteria, or classrooms. Teachers become too busy being disciplinarians to teach; administrators become too busy being policemen and policewomen to be instructional leaders; or the recalcitrant students are so passively resistant to learning and school culture that ambitious attempts to reach them seem futile.

Much of the money that is gained from state and federal sources because these recalcitrant students have been lured back to school will be spent on security measures such as security personnel, hall monitors, metal detectors, and armed off duty police officers. It is extremely difficult to teach people against their will.

## Why Do They Drop Out in the First Place?

Perhaps it would be wise to look at the most common reasons why students have poor attendance or choose to dropout of school. Students have poor attendance because they are disinterested or afraid to attend, embarrassed to attend, have reasons to stay out of school that seem more important or feel better than the reasons to stay in school. When one or more of these reasons for poor attendance becomes overwhelming or extremely compelling, the students often become dropouts. Once students drop out of school, they rarely complete, even if they do return to school.

Students that have poor attendance because they are disinterested or afraid to attend usually have problems with the learning process, individual teachers, or with other students that create problems at school.

- Disinterested students say they are bored because classes are not interesting, too difficult, or that this or that teacher does not like them.
- Students who are afraid often avoid school to avoid the bullies and intimidators. These students seldom report their fears to school officials or anyone else; it is simply a silent irritant that only disappears when they are absent. Schools where discipline issues are not consistently confronted and enforced make the atmosphere fertile for fear. Students once fearful of attending school hardly ever experience a return of the courage that it takes for them to resume school attendance.
- Students who are embarrassed to attend school usually have issues that involve problems with socio-economic conditions or problems with dysfunctional family situations. Sometimes the student feels self-conscious about his or her clothes, shoes, hair, or some other external concern. The student may not have money to buy items that are necessary for school attendance. Sometimes students are not prepared academically because, the night before, too many disruptive occurrences interfered with their attention to schoolwork. These conditions occur most often because of ineffective parenting, sometimes because of negligence or sometimes because of circumstances beyond the parents' control.
- Some students have reasons that seem more important, or they feel better than the reasons to attend school. Many of the female students discontinue attendance because motherhood has become an overpowering concern. This happens most often with teen mothers that have multiple children. Some of the boys have intense desires to be independent and get jobs that bring irresistible, immediate gratification. Sometimes young people become engulfed with car-support; the maintenance and possession of an automobile becomes of paramount concern. Also, and most distressing are the young people that get involved with drugs and alcohol to the extent that it rules their existence.

# Engulfed

When the above situations engulf a student and that student does not have access to safety nets that student will almost certainly drop out of school. Some people might argue that if the classes at school were not boring, or if the teachers were more dynamic, or if there were this or that new program, reluctant students would be more compelled to attend. Whatever the argument, under current conditions students that have attendance problems regularly create problems for the inner workings of the school on days when they decide to be present. Parents, concerned community members, politicians, business people, and church leaders need to take a serious and soul-searching look at these issues and consider which of the situations mentioned could be better addressed through other agencies. Aside from the disinterest and fear concerns, educators might be hard-pressed to have a positive or effective impact on the other two concerns of those that have poor attendance or that drop out.

Perhaps state and federal government nurture this condition by offering money to school districts based on attendance. Many school districts will do almost anything to receive the extra money the added attendance levels will bring to the school district. But, what happens to the school when those students that would rather dropout or attend occasionally return to school? Maybe a better criteria for receiving government funds might be some formula that takes into consideration the socio-economic condition of the attendance area and results on state assessment instruments would be a better way to determine how the money would be distributed.

# Impact of Recalcitrant Students on the Schools

First, special rules and guidelines must be developed so that they can maintain some level of success (lowered standards). Second, behavioral expectations have to be altered so that the recalcitrant students can make it through days without getting caught in the discipline system (Educators have to "look the other way"). Third and most harmful, the students that come to school to learn become second-class citizens because most of the time and attention of the adults are going to the recalcitrant students; being in class with recalcitrant students is a challenge for all involved. Often, learning takes a backseat to discipline issues in classes that have just a few recalcitrant students; many of the students that intended to give effective effort find futility in this and often simply give up because they see that the behavior of the recalcitrant students is what gets the adult attention.

Most people do not want to give up on the chance that some students with poor attendance may have a change of heart and become a student with regular attendance. Data however does not support this line of thinking; exhaustive efforts have been embraced to bring the drop-outs back to school but the amount of success does not equal the effort and resources extended. Most people can agree that education is a gift that adult humans give to their children. The energy and concern toward education would bring greater return if it were directed to the students and families that appreciate the gift.

- State and federal funding might be better spent if it were based on the academic achievement of students. Perhaps students and families would be more inclined to have greater appreciation for the gift of an education if effort instead of simple attendance was rewarded.

- Parents and students might have more respect for educators if free breakfast and lunch were based on students actually passing classes and acquiring credits in school rather than just showing up.
- The court system, the welfare system, and the Social Security system might be less abused if judgments and pay-outs involving children were based on academic effort and achievement rather than simple attendance.

People have more respect for themselves when they are appreciated, held in high regard, and rewarded for actual work that they do and achievements that they have accomplished rather than being given handouts; lessons from the Great Depression should have taught us this.

## QUO Process Shifts the Focus to Those Students That Attend

Within the ideology of QUO Process, students that attend school to learn would be the main priority. Interventions would be used to attempt salvation for recalcitrant students without relying on special privileges and softened standards. When quality, unity, and order are required of students it also compels the same from parents and educators; QUO Process raises the bar for everyone and initially some people will not like that.

> **Within the ideology of QUO Process, students that attend school to learn would be the main priority.**

# Chapter 5
# The Nemesis of the Low-Achiever

The constant "nemisis of low-achieving students" is complex and comes from at least three directions:

## 1. Cycle of Pain

Children that continuously have low academic achievement are caught deep within the "Cycle of Pain." These children generally have easy access to **the intoxicants of life** including: illegal drugs, alcohol, smoking, recreational sexual activity, and other negative endeavors. Steadily exposed to these intoxicants, these children become addicted and crave even more exposure to life's intoxicants. Children in the cycle of pain are often taught a **distorted set of values** by adults that grew up in the pain cycle. Values expressing that it is acceptable to break rules, slide through guidelines, and ignore common civility dominate the lives of children caught within the cycle of pain.

Having a steady diet of distorted values leaves students little resolve to achieve a strong education foundation. In their thinking, classes are too difficult, there is too much homework, teachers are too demanding, and the rules in school are too strict. Any event that can be used to validate that school will not lead to success immediately comes to the forefront as **evidence that gaining an education is not worthwhile.**

## 2. Lack of Progressive Development

This idea of the senselessness of gaining education is further exacerbated when the students engulfed in the pain cycle witness a lack of progressive development. When it is empirical that social injustices where American-blacks are the last hired and first fired, locked out of promotions, hold parallel positions with American-whites but are second-guessed and held in lower regard, then American-black students become distressed. Further, when compassionate assistance to students is non-existent from the educators within schools—where teachers work only the contractual days, and too few of them coach, sponsor clubs, arrive early, stay after school to help tutor students, or attend extra-curricular activities to support the students, American-black students feel uncared for.

When students witness a lack of social injustice and compassionate assistance, American-black students become void of self-determination and either stop trying or do not even begin trying. The students become angry as they move further into the pain cycle. Their anger becomes even more intense as evidence surfaces revealing that the educators working with them really do not care about them.

## 3. Achievement Gap

It becomes difficult for American-black students to secure academic success and decrease the gap in achievement when so much is against them. As discussed in Chapter 2, institutionalized disincentive, internalized self-doubt, and the covenant of neglect work together to cause the gap in achievement.

**When the achievement gap connects with a lack of progressive development, poverty awaits American-black students.** Impending poverty is like the theme music in a horror movie; the audience braces itself for the next horrific event when the music begins to play.

> **Impending poverty is like the theme music in a horror movie; the audience braces itself for the next horrific event when the music begins to play.**

As the negatives continue to build, American-black students can almost *feel* the trappings of poverty engulfing them.

**When the achievement gap connects with the cycle of pain, American-black students can sense that they have no safety nets** and know that they will certainly be locked out of mainstream America where the American dream exists.

## Some Do Overcome

When the pain cycle, accompanied by a lack of progressive development, is joined by the achievement gap, American-black students truly face formidable odds. Nevertheless some American-black students reveal absolute strength of character, determination, and forthrightness, achieving in spite of the obstacles. Those who do succeed are heroes in their own right. They are an American phenomenon and deserve to be protected and honored. Educators, colleges, places of employment, politicians, and the military would be wise to hold them in the highest regard.

## Change Course

Educators and adults in the families of American-black students can change the course of the downward spiral inherent in the nemesis of low-achieving students. Educators and the adults in the families of school children can take the lead in meeting the needs of the young people to help them learn at higher rates. Educators can take this as a challenge to their professionalism. There is great satisfaction in knowing that a place is better off or people are better off because a team of educators made a difference. There are plenty of examples that show improvement has occurred in a place, an area, or among people when a special person or group of people arrived and implemented different or new strategies. Presidents, businessmen, religious leaders, doctors, lawyers, coaches, and educators have done this and it can be accomplished again with the obliteration of the nemesis of low-achieving students.

**To obliterate the nemesis, schools need a structure** that is predictable, but flexible; consistent, but adaptable; and firm, but accommodating. **Schools need a new organizational system and a new operational structure.** An effective organizational structure would be one where students and their families are nurtured by the educators that interact with the students. The best organizational systems are embedded with avenues of collaboration along with internal checks and balances. The operational structure concepts are the ideas that should drive everything that occurs in the school.

# Chapter 6
# QUO: A Framework for Quality, Unity, and Order

## *A Common Language to Get to the "Green"*

*To embrace unity, those that prescribe to "Green Culture" value humility, teamwork, love for country and citizenship, courage, loyalty, religion and religious freedom, family, respect for the elderly, compassion, and gratitude.*

Modified from *The Good Book*, by Bill Jenkins

Almost all of the low achievers will endure poverty and limited opportunities. The realities that accompany this condition usually create volatile hostilities within many low achievers. Lessons from history reveal that a poor, hostile populous that has external similarities such as color, religion, and race, which are different from the majority population, creates a negative psychological situation. American society depends on schools to face these problems, identify specific at-risk students, and implement strategies for resolution. Obviously, continuing to deliver education in the same old way is not the answer; a different approach is needed. In effect, educators have an opportunity to build new metaphorical schoolhouses of intellectual transformation.

QUO Process will help members of the Learning Triad (parents, educators, and students) work together as a team to navigate the school environment and gain a general understanding of the "No Child Left Behind" Act, school improvement mandates, and initiatives. Further, the QUO Process will help those within the Learning Triad realize solid school practices and give them a common language to use when talking with each other to gain the best education for students that will help them earn a place within green culture—social, economic, and political prosperity, personal power, and the access to a high resource, American-dream existence.

**The ideas and concepts that create ORDER** in the green culture is basic in American thought:

- Respect for authority and the rights and property of others
- Justice and fair play
- Obeying the rules

- Life and human dignity

(Modified from *The Good Book*, by Bill Jenkins)

**To embrace UNITY,** those that prescribe to green culture value:
- Humility
- Love for country and citizenship
- Courage
- Loyalty
- Religion and religious freedom
- Family
- Respect for the elderly
- Compassion
- Gratitude

**To cultivate QUALITY,** those within the green culture respect:
- Knowledge
- Taking care of the environment
- Contributing to society
- Virtue
- Honesty and integrity in speech and deed
- Diligent and honest work
- Taking personal responsibility

## Using the QUO Process to Reorganize Public Schools

The National High School Alliance released "A Call to Action" Transforming High School for All Youth." A framework of six core principles and recommended strategies for guiding leaders at all levels in the complex process of transforming the traditional, comprehensive high school. The six core principles cited as "inter-related and non-negotiable" are:
1. Personalized learning environment
2. Academic engagement of all children
3. Empowered educators
4. Accountable leaders
5. Engaged community & youth
6. Integrated systems of high standards, curriculum, instruction, assessments and academic supports beyond the school day

The QUO Process offers America a practical solution; a different approach to education. The QUO Process is named for the improvements it brings to the school environment: **Q**uality, **U**nity, and **O**rder. QUO offers a framework for creating necessary new structures to encourage the Learning Triad (educators, students, and parents) to gain quality, unity, and order by embracing the following strategies:

To Introduce **Order,** Protect the Learning Environment by:
- Embracing "Parallel Supervision"

68

- Improving communication within the Learning Triad of students, educators, families and community members

To Develop **Unity**, Implement a Systemic Learning Cycle by:
- Authenticating the curriculum
- Implementing Assessment-Based Instruction (ABI)

To Assure **Quality**, Manage Direct Data by:
- Identifying struggling students and high achievers
- Creating recovery techniques for struggling students and enrichments for high-achieving students

# QUO Process

| Custodial Component | Academic Component |
|---|---|
| ***ORDER:* Protect the Learning Environment** Improved Communication Parallel Supervision | ***UNITY:* Systematic Learning Cycle** Authenticate the Curriculum Assessment Based Instruction |

**QUALITY: Manage Direct Data**
For the Custodial and Academic Components
Identify students that struggle and students that excel
Introduce strategies for recovery and enichment

# Chapter 7
# Implementing the QUO Process

The most effective way to implement the QUO Process is to include the entire school district in its development. Both vertical and horizontal articulation is needed where those within the Learning Triad communicate and collaborate about the QUO Process, across each level of education—primary, intermediate, and secondary. School districts would need to establish a three-part system of organization; facilitation teams, levels looping (triangular looping at the elementary level and core curriculum teams looping at the secondary level), and collaborative cooperatives.

## School Systems and Structures Needed to Implement QUO

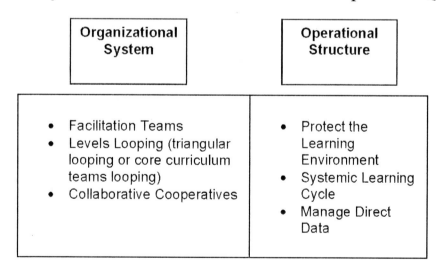

| Organizational System | Operational Structure |
|---|---|
| • Facilitation Teams<br>• Levels Looping (triangular looping or core curriculum teams looping)<br>• Collaborative Cooperatives | • Protect the Learning Environment<br>• Systemic Learning Cycle<br>• Manage Direct Data |

## FACILITATION TEAMS

Facilitation Teams provide leadership within the district. At the building level principals could seek to have not more than 20 staff members on the Facilitation Team. The principals of buildings could invite the core curriculum department heads to be members of the Facilitation Team then have a vote on the faculty for the remaining members. Principals could also invite at least one parent and one community member (not a parent of a student attending that particular school) to be members of the leadership team and comprise the Facilitation Team at the building levels.

Principals would look to the Facilitation Team in their buildings for direction. The Facilitation Team in each building would make determinations concerning the strategies to be used in each of the components of QUO Process. The Facilitation Team for each building would decide at least one approach the staff would use for all components and strategies of QUO Process. Principals would share the plan with the superintendent for approval and use the plan as the mandate for administrative direction.

Each building level administrator would represent the leadership team of his or her building at planning meetings of the district level Facilitation Team. At the district level leadership meetings, it would be collectively determined how the central office could best facilitate individual buildings in their efforts to implement QUO Process. District level Facilitation Teams would devise ways to be sensitive to coaches, maintenance, custodians, school nurses, secretaries, monitors, and cafeteria workers in the strategies for QUO Process. The plans devised by the Facilitation Team at the district level and at the building level could be used by administrators as a mandate for direction.

# LEVELS LOOPING

**Elementary Level:** To administer Quo Process school districts could implement a system of matriculation where students at the elementary level would be engaged in triangular looping. **Triangular Looping** would consist of having a teacher receive a class of kindergarteners and stay with the same students for three years, grades K-2. A different teacher would take charge of the class for the next three years, grades 3-5. The two teachers, one primary and one intermediate, would form a team and plan together to lay out a plan for the students that will take them through elementary school. At middle and high schools **Core Curriculum** teams **of teachers** would usher cohorts of students through their secondary education. **The main objectives of the triangular and core curriculum teams of teachers would be to nurture the humanity of the students, demystify the academic code so that the students can learn and gain high achievement on standardized tests, and model and require civil behavior.**

**Intermediate Level:** The intermediate level teachers could team with the primary level teachers from whom their students come. The intermediate level teachers could also be on a team with all of the other intermediate level teachers in the building. This scenario could also hold true for the primary level teachers. The high school cohort could team with the middle school teacher teams that teach the middle school cohort; and the core curriculum team teachers could also be part of the team of the subject matter departments as they relate to the teachers individually as well. This would also hold true for the middle school teachers that shepherd the students on the middle school cohort. Consequently, the teachers could have a system for collaboration about the students and for collaboration about subject matter and teaching techniques.

**Middle School Level:** At the middle school the top 10 percent of the students arriving in sixth grade would be identified and placed into the **Honors Cohort**, received by a team or teams of core curriculum teachers and shepherded through three years of middle school.

Administrators could make sure that the top 10 percent or more of the American-black students in attendance would be included in the cohort. The cohort of students would be divided into sections of no more than 120 students each; the larger the school, the larger the cohort. Each cohort of students would be shepherded by one core curriculum team of teachers. The remaining sixth grade students would be randomly divided and assigned to core curriculum teams that would shepherd the students for three years.

**High School Level:** At the high school level the top 10 percent of the students arriving in ninth grade would be identified and placed into the Honors Cohort received by a team or teams of core curriculum teachers and shepherded through four years of high school. A cohort of students would consist of no more than 120 students. Each cohort of students would be shepherded by one core curriculum team of teachers (Most of these students would probably be the same students that were in the middle school cohort.) The remaining ninth grade students would be randomly divided into **Random Cohorts** and assigned to core curriculum teams that would shepherd the students for four years.

The teachers at every level would comply with an organization design inherent within QUO Process. Protecting the learning environment pertains to the governance and safety of the school community, implementing a systemic learning cycle focusing on pedagogy, curriculum and assessment, and attention to managing data and instituting academic support initiatives spotlight data collection and response to the data. The overriding concept of the QUO Process is that teachers use authenticated curriculum to deliver lessons.

Teachers would use teacher-designed tests and performance event assignments, based on authenticated curriculum to measure a student's progress. Teachers would then use quarterly common assessments as diagnostics to determine where students are in relation to the authenticated curriculum and the other students in the school at the same grade level. The testing would be used to prescribe strategies to be used to help students learn more and improve so that when they take the state and national standardized tests they will be prepared.

**Research suggests that students often have greater academic success, especially at elementary levels, when they and their parents have good relationships with the educators.** When considering this, it might be smart to make the creation of relationships imbedded within the very fabric of the entire school district. The formation of levels looping would institute a scheme that would help the formation of relationships because students and parents would have the same teacher or teachers several years in succession.

In contemporary school districts elementary school students might have six teachers in six years of kindergarten through fifth grade. Even with conventional looping the students and families might have to interact

> Teachers would have the opportunity to take ownership for the development of students because there will be more of a personal time investment.

with at least five teachers in a student's elementary school experience. Within the triangular looping concept however, a family might have only two teachers to get to know over a six-year period. Students, families, and teachers would have a better possibility to get to know each other more intimately. Teachers would have the opportunity to take ownership for the development of students because there will be more of a personal time investment.

# Triangular Looping Builds Relationships

Triangular looping creates an atmosphere where the two teachers that will teach the same students in the primary and intermediate grades, the teams of four teachers in the core curriculum that will usher students through the middle school years, and the teams of four teachers that will shepherd students through the first three years of high school could collaborate *vertically* to determine how they would implement the QUO Process as the students grow and mature.

At the elementary level, for example, the teacher of third graders would team with the teacher of kindergarteners. Together they would decide how the QUO Process would be implemented for the students that they teach. Together they would devise a plan so one would know what the other was doing with the students and know at what grade level materials would be covered.

The teachers would exchange classes at different times throughout the year. In this way, the teachers would actually have a six-year connection to the students and families. The teachers could also form student tutoring partners where the students in the higher grades would study with the students of the lower grades. The third graders would tutor the kindergarteners and continue the relationship for three years so that by the time the kindergarteners entered the ninth grade there would be seniors at the high school that they know and have learned with.

## Core Curriculum Teams

Triangular looping would occur at the elementary school level while core curriculum teams would occur at the secondary level. When students enter the sixth grade the top 10 percent would be assigned to a team or teams of four core curriculum teachers. The students would stay with the same team of teachers for the three years that they attend middle school. The core curriculum team members could collaborate with each other to create a plan designed to usher students from sixth through eighth grade. Within this plan teachers would make certain that students academically move through school learning "the right stuff."

At the high school level the students in the top 10 percent would be placed on a core curriculum team or teams upon entry into the ninth grade. Once received, teachers would stay with the students for three years. The teachers that comprise each team would create plans to shepherd students for three years making certain that the students learn the right stuff. The teachers could also assign student tutoring partners where the students in the second year would study with the students in the first year and the students in the third year would study with the students in the second year. Furthermore, teachers could encourage students to form study circles where teachers would show students how to study together regularly.

# COLLABORATIVE COOPERATIVES
# BASED ON CURRICULUM

Collaborative cooperatives are where elementary school teachers that teach the same grade levels would collaborate and secondary **teachers that teach in the same core curriculum subject areas would collaborate.** The objective of the collaboration would be to study the state descriptors and ACT preparation information so that everyone understands what students need to know to perform well on the state test. Further, teachers could take inventory of course offerings, in some cases to streamline choices for subject matter and in other cases to add courses to make certain that information needed to cover state descriptors are available. The inventory could also analyze sequencing to make sure that necessary courses are attended by students, in a timely matter, before the test is given. Collaborative cooperatives would be the main group of teachers that plan, determine, and develop the curriculum for a school district and for individual schools.

Each building within school districts embracing QUO Process would have a collaborative cooperative. One person from every grade level from all elementary schools in the district and one person from each core curriculum level would represent the middle and high schools. One to four teachers from each building level collaborative cooperative would represent their buildings to the central office to comprise the district level collaborative cooperative. The district level collaborative cooperatives would review all curriculum items and suggest a district-wide curriculum initiative.

When Facilitation Teams, levels looping, and collaborative cooperative teams of teachers plan together, students and teachers who are new to buildings will have smooth transitions. Furthermore, the strategies and plans developed could be introduced as the school improvement plan for each building. Two or more subject-specific areas in secondary schools could target skills such as reading comprehension and math for intensified concentration. This cross-curriculum articulation might help students see connections between the different segments of the curriculum.

# HOW TO MEASURE

As the teacher teams plan implementation of the QUO Process guidelines of MCER could be followed to structure plans made. Teacher teams could agree that every strategy made pertaining to the QUO Process have MCER:

- the capacity to be *measured*
- the capacity to be *compared* with the results of what was done in the past, what has occurred at the state level, and what was done on other parallel teams. Therefore, comparisons must be possible both horizontally and vertically.
- the capacity to be *evaluated*
- the expectation of *revision* based on the measurements, comparisons, and evaluations

The guidelines of MCER (M-Sir) give the strategies structure and discipline. By applying these guidelines, teacher teams can make data-driven changes yearly that will help improve methods used to implement the QUO Process and increase student learning.

Currently, in education, educators endeavor to hire good people, but once hired they are often sent to buildings and left to prosper or flounder on their own. The QUO Process offers educators a framework for the development of plans unique to individual buildings and teacher teams within school districts. The QUO Process provides a structure for Collaborative School Transformation while promoting academic excellence.

# Part Four
# To Introduce Order, Protect the Learning Environment

- Establish Parallel Supervision

- Improve communication within the Learning Triad of students, educators, families/community members

# Chapter 8
# Call to Order

*"Fifty years after Brown, the nation still has not figured out how to educate all its children. African-Americans, on average, start kindergarten academically behind whites, and the gap grows during elementary school. The ripple effect carries into high school and beyond. Although blacks and whites enter college at similar rates, 36 percent of whites graduate with a four-year degree, compared with only 18 percent of blacks. Black jobless rates are higher than white's and black income is lower. The achievement gap between whites and blacks remains an affront to the national creed, that all are created equal. To reach that goal, schools must find ways to prevent disorder and indifference from overwhelming education."*

Julian E. Barnes. "Unequal Education: Now the Focus Shifts from Integration to Achievement for All." *U.S. News & World Report.* March 22-29 2004, pages 68-69.

### The Staff Development Committee—Opportunity Missed
The phone rang three times before she answered. Ted Wohlfarth, founder and executive director of EnTeam, an organization dedicated to developing win-win collaborative relationships, and I heard her talking to other people in the room before she acknowledged us. (Ted and I provide staff development for schools and school districts to help them embrace Collaborative School Transformation.)

*"Hello,"* she said.

*"Hello, Allison,"* Ted began. *"I have you on speaker because Ed Harris is here with me. Are we calling at a good time?"*

*"Yes, I think everyone is here on my end,"* Allison said. *"Bill, Maxine, Catherine, and Ranesha are here with me."*

We all said a jovial hello in unison.

Ted had talked with Allison earlier and they decided on an agreeable time when we could make the conference call to the entire Staff Development Committee from Perdition High School. The state placed Perdition High School along with the other two district high schools, on the state watch list because of low performance. The Staff Development Committee would decide whether or not Ted and I would work with their staff on the QUO Process. As curriculum director from the district level administration, Allison sat on the staff development committee at all three high schools.

*"We have looked over the proposal and it looks pretty good,"* Allison said. *"But we have a couple of questions."*

*"Great, ask about whatever you would like to know,"* Ted responded.

*"We notice that you prefer to have the first interaction between you and the staff be a three-day workshop?"* Allison said.

*"Yes,"* Ted replied. *"It takes about three days for a staff to internalize the information from the components so that they can gain a critical mass for buy in."*

*"Hi, Ted and Ed, this is Bill."* Ted and I said hello to Bill almost in unison. *"So what you two are offering is a school reform model?"* Bill asked.

*"Not exactly Bill,"* I said. *"We like to make a distinction between what we advocate and school reform. We like to speak in terms of educators working together to transform schools rather than school reform. School reform models generally select one facet of school functions and focus on that. We think that this is like asking a builder to build a house and when the builder is finished all that stands is a bathroom. We believe that when a builder is employed to build a house, the whole structure should be constructed. That is why we believe in educators working together to transform the entire school, not simply addressing a piece of the problem."*

Ted and I heard lots of conversation on the other end as if what I said caught the attention of the group.

*"Hi, Ted and Ed, Maxine here; I am the chairperson of the math department and we are having problems with students not doing so well in, say, Algebra 1 the first semester then moving on to Algebra 2 in the second semester and falling further behind. Is there something you can give us that will help us with this problem?"*

*"No, but we can initiate conversations and engage in activities that will help you and members of your department work together as a team and to make some*

*decisions that will help you come away with a few strategies to confront those issues and help students learn,"* I said.

Ted and I heard more energized discussion through the phone.

*"Hi, Ted and Ed; this is Ranesha. How ya'll doing today?"*

Ted and I looked at each other with a smile as we said hello. We recognized right away by her friendly tone and accent that she was an American-black member of the committee.

*"I am a special education teacher and most of my IEP's (Special Education Students with individualized education plans) are African-American boys,"* Ranesha said. *"They seem dead against learning anything that is school-related. We have trouble keeping them out of trouble. I think that much of the problem is due to boredom with the classes. Do you address this during the workshop?"*

*"Ranesha, we try to have the teachers practice several cooperative learning techniques and EnTeam frame games that the teachers can add to their arsenal of strategies to use with their students as we proceed through the three days of workshop,"* Ted replied. *"But we also endeavor to engage people in discussion about how to address all four learning styles in each of their lessons when they present to students. The students have to believe that the teachers are teaching them something that is going to be helpful to them, something that they can use."*

With silence on the other end of the phone, Ted and I waited for more questions.

*"We are a little worried that the central office will balk at the cost of the workshops,"* Finally Catherine spoke. *"Are you willing to negotiate?"*

*"We understand that school budgets are often tight,"* I smiled as I spoke and said. *"We are trying to do something to help save public education so we will work with districts."*

*"We could stretch our time with you over a longer period,"* Ted added. *"We realize that you may want some follow-up with our facilitators who are less expensive to have on campus than having the two of us would be."*

Ted had a few questions for them concerning the demographics of the district and the amount of previous staff development and how teachers received it. They answered our questions readily, but Ranesha put it best.

*"The bottom line is that our students are not performing well, especially the African-American students, and we need to do something about it,"* she said.

*"Now we have tried all kinds of school reform and it has not helped us. We have had school within a school. We have tried establishing a ninth grade center. We have tried the Coalition of Essential Schools. And we are still pretty much working in anarchy. We are getting a new superintendent next year, but we definitely need something that works."*

Ted and I heard the others in the background voicing agreement. Allison told us that she would present the idea to their Board of Education and get back with us in two weeks. We all said a cordial good bye and ended the call.

Ted and I visited with over 100 educators from the Perdition School District for three days of staff development. The participating educators in the three-day sessions gave rave reviews on the evaluation sheets. The teachers were ready to get started with the QUO Process in the next school year; however, unfortunately a new superintendent arrived and the process ended.

## Teachers Don't Feel Supported by the Administration

Educators in many American school districts experience the same feelings and frustrations as the teachers at Perdition. When Ted and I visited Perdition High School the initial conversations during the staff development workshop revolved around the teachers' frustration with what they called, **"a failure by the administration, at the building and district levels to address discipline issues."** After spending three days with

> **The teachers felt as if the administrators did not value them enough to be consistent with discipline.**

the teachers at Perdition, we discovered that much of what the administrators interpreted as teacher apathy was actually feelings of neglect and non-support. The teachers felt as if the administrators did not value them enough to be consistent with discipline.

The teachers were feeling as if the administrators would "cave-in" to the students and their parents; discipline was not consistent and in the view of the teachers, at times actually non-existent.

Students that give effective effort and parents that are supportive are wonderful to work with; but what we learned at Perdition is that many teachers are probably slow to engage when they feel unsupported and left to endure disrespect and powerlessness in the face of recalcitrant youngsters and their enabling parents.

The teachers at Perdition reinforced the notion that for the QUO Process to be most effective, order must be achieved first.

# Chapter 9
# Establishing Parallel Supervision

*"Great schools have a zero tolerance attitude toward discipline infractions. They eliminate warnings and make a real connection between actions and consequences. It is the single most important lesson to learn for students that grow up in chaotic homes and neighborhoods. In great schools expectations in all areas are high; students are expected to master a core set of basic skills in the core curriculum."*

Abigail and Stephan Thernstrom, *No Excuses*, Closing the Racial Gap in Learning

### "My Baby Dead."

It was a small church in a neighborhood where American-blacks lived. As I drove toward my destination I was saddened as I passed through several blocks of buildings that looked as if they were transplants from a war zone in some far away place. Buildings stood with just a shell, boarded windows and doors. It was a place that one would not volunteer to visit at night.

As I entered the church I saw several students that I had seen around school. It occurred to me that all of them probably lived near the church which would have placed them outside the school district where I was principal. It became obvious that the students were sneaking into the district. Their parents were probably sending them to the school where I was principal to keep them away from the gangs and violence. This had not worked for Thugerty James.

I shook hands with Thugerty's relatives as I walked through the door to take my place in line at the rear of the church. I looked to the front of the small church to see a lady dressed in black sitting on the front pew being embraced by two elderly women dressed in white. The casket lay in front of them draped in black with candles on each side beside recent pictures of Thugerty before he died.

About 35 people were inside the church and three or four were waiting at the door to say hello to the family member greeters before going inside. People were handling the occasion in different ways. Aside from an occasional spine chilling, outcry by Thugerty's mother, some people were crying, some were quiet, but all were solemn. Family and friends were sad that Thugerty was dead.

I looked toward the front of the room and again caught sight of Thugerty's mother, Fussalot Enablton. I was lost in thought when I was startled by Mrs. Enablton's outburst of agony. The jolt made me remember back one year prior when I held a conference with Mrs. Enablton and her son, Thugerty James.

Thugerty had been suspended for fighting after school in the spring of the year. I asked his mother to come for a re-entry conference when he returned after the 10 days out. Thugerty had been involved in four fights during the year and I explained to his mother that there were rumors among the students that Thugerty was gang-banging and using and selling drugs. I explained that Thugerty had not actually been *caught* with the drugs at school but that school security personnel suspected that he was using and selling at school.

I remembered that Thugerty's mother was very defensive when I told her about the suspicions and rumors. She began yelling at me and saying that I was allowing the security people to pick on her son. She said that the staff members had labeled Thugerty and were scarring him for life.

Mrs. Enableton told Thugerty that they were leaving and they both bolted toward the door. I said, *"Mrs. Enableton, we need to confront this situation now so that we can head it off; or I predict that we may be having one of our future meetings in a jail, the hospital or the funeral home."*

Mrs. Enableton turned to me and said, *"I don't need you or any of the other damn teachers around here telling me how to raise my son and I wish that all of you would stay out of our business. I'm going to the school board on your ass."*

After her remarks (which she delivered as loudly as she could) she and Thugerty left the office. Thugerty returned the next day but Mrs. Enableton never came to the school again. I spoke with her on the phone several times but we never spoke face to face after that. I did not know what to expect as my place in line moved closer to the casket and her at the front of the church.

The news article about Thugerty's death was short but concise. The article explained that Thugerty had been shot six times in a drive-by. The authorities were sure that it was a gang-related drug-deal-gone-bad incident. The shooting had occurred late Thursday evening on the north side of town. No suspects were detained.

The closer I moved to the casket the more concerned I became about coming face-to-face with Thugerty's mother, I dreaded her reaction. Our conversations became less strained as the months passed but we talked almost every week interacting because of some problem Thugerty was having at school with staff members or other students. Thugerty's grades had gone from Honor Roll to the pits in a short few months. Thugerty's father, Loelafe James, never married Thugerty's mother and left them completely two months before our final conference was held. Some people in the community said that his father's leaving had caused something to snap in Thugerty's brain and that he never recovered.

When I arrived at the front of the church Mrs. Enableton looked at me as if she had seen a ghost—as if I was a long lost person whom everyone had thought dead. Her face went blank as she stared at me; then suddenly she burst into tears and flung her arms around me. I embraced her tightly and it was as if I could feel her grief; the pain like no other that a parent feels that has to bury a child.

She glared into my eyes and said softly, *"Mr. Harris my baby dead."*

Attention to parallel supervision may have saved Thugerty's life. Students need to understand that educators and the adult caregivers are working together to help the student become successful. Students can gain a real sense of consistency when they realize that their primary caregiver and educators have parallel behavioral and academic expectations.

## Checklist For Failure

Too many parents today have distorted views about raising children and often confuse being a child's parent with being a child's friend. Children already have plenty of opportunity to make friends at school and in the neighborhood, but often have only one opportunity to have a parent. When parents opt to become friends to their children instead of parents, they are setting their children up for failure.

In his satirical book, *How To Rear Inferior Black Children*, William Jenkins gives examples of what some American-black parents do that sets their children on the road to failure. According to the Jenkins book a black parent seeking to raise inferior children could:

- ✓ Make sure that your black children are yours all by yourself.
- ✓ Fail to acquire a high school education.
- ✓ Make sure that the father of your child is nowhere around, and you like it that way.
- ✓ Never read to your child or encourage reading.
- ✓ Make sure that you never take your children to a zoo, museum, opera, park, or any other cultural venues.
- ✓ Make sure that your children's studies of people are limited to themselves and other black people.
- ✓ Refrain from getting involved with the education of your children.
- ✓ Make sure that your children rarely see anyone going to a responsible job, but instead are surrounded by people who sell drugs and each other.

✓ Never help your children with their homework.

✓ Allow your children to do whatever they please and have no place at home where they are to study.

✓ Make sure that your children never hear the word God unless it's followed by damn.

✓ Make sure that everything that your children are given is without strings attached.

✓ Make sure your children do not get disciplined by you or anyone else.

✓ Make sure that you tell your children every bad thing that you can think of about white people and America.

✓ Give your children no hope for the future and explain to them that they do not have to listen to constructive criticism from anyone, not even Bill Cosby.

✓ Make sure that your children dress and carry themselves in ways that will cause the rest of society to be suspicious of them, afraid of them or both.

# GETTING THE LEARNING TRIAD TO EMBRACE PARALLEL SUPERVISON

- When parents and educators cooperate and collaborate to help students extend academically, students will understand that it is possible to reach full potential when they comply with guidelines and rules.

> **When the school and the adults in a student's family are in cadence, the real winner is the student.**

- When the school and the adults in a student's family are in cadence, the real winner is the student.

- When students achieve academically, educators can trust that parents are implementing strategies at home that cause the students to prosper and experience success.

- When families can trust educators to initiate progressive academic plans they can be sure that students will progress toward success and achievement at school.

## No Surprises

No one likes surprises about serious issues. Here is a copy of the 2004 Cahokia High School Principal's Newsletter that was sent to the parents to explain what they should expect from the school concerning the expectations for their children's behavior and to request their commitment to practicing parallel supervision at home:

*Dear Parents,*

*Cahokia High School students are expected to represent their families with vigor. We realize that the students at Cahokia High School come from families that believe in high moral values, honor, and character. Cahokia High School students can be as dignified and as focused on academic achievement as students anywhere. Not only is this possible, but nothing less will be accepted at Cahokia High School.*

*Cahokia High School is transforming into a place where parents can send their children because they know that the school has a safe, no-nonsense environment with an atmosphere that is conducive to personal development and achievement; a place where students will receive an excellent education and take an "academic back seat" to no one. The students at Cahokia High School can achieve and they will achieve because that is what parents and school personnel require. When parents and educators work together there is no reason why the students at Cahokia High School cannot be among the best and brightest students in Illinois, with some of the best test scores, grade point averages, and behavior in the entire country.*

*A strategy that can facilitate the parent and educator partnership is the implementation of **parallel supervision**. Within this strategy parents agree to implement the four components of parallel supervision at home and the educators agree to introduce the four components at school. Within this plan both parents and educators would:*

- *Establish behavioral boundaries and high academic expectations*
- *Create systems of support and monitoring*
- *Exact consequences for non-compliance*
- *Give praise, recognition, and privileges when students comply*

*At school we educators set guidelines for behavior, protect the rules of individual teachers, and require common civility. Educators also press for academic achievement, demand that students aspire for Cs or better, require students to give consistent effective effort, and insist on punctuality and regular attendance. To support students, educators at Cahokia High School have established an Academic Lab, offer student tutors for students in need, and make available intensified assistance with specialists in reading and computer software in math. To monitor student progress, educators have initiated an Academic Watch List, a behavior checklist, and student classification guidelines.*

*We educators have instituted escalating consequences and a variety of ways to recognize, praise, and give privileges to students that comply with boundaries and expectations. We are asking that parents do the same at home so that the supervision will be not only consistent, but parallel and the same general procedures that occur at home also occur at school. In this way there can be no mistake about it among students; **parents and educators will do what it takes to help students achieve success.***

*Parents need to expect that teachers will steadily raise expectations in all classes. Students that are trying to understand and trying to do the work but need additional help and explanation will be assigned to Academic Lab that meets on Monday, Tuesday, Wednesday, and Thursday afternoons after school from 2:00 to 3:55. Students that refuse academic services by not doing class work during the day, or not doing homework will be sent to after school detention by the teachers and parents will be contacted. If the student continues to refuse academic services he or she will eventually be sent to in-school suspension by administrators.*

*The staff at Cahokia High School is dedicated to preparing your youngsters to be dignified, smart, responsible, intelligent, resourceful leaders and we are committed to being relentless in that effort.*

*Sincerely,*

*Dr. Ed Harris*
*Principal Cahokia High School*

Individual classrooms are where the rubber meets the road in education and no learning can be accomplished in those individual classrooms until teachers make it clear that the classroom is a place of learning and distracting behaviors will not be tolerated. Teachers must relentlessly confront any behavior transgressions every time they occur. It must be made clear that teachers will use a variety of strategies to keep their classrooms free from negative interference.

## What Teachers Can Require of Students to Gain Parallel Supervision:

- Attention must be given to human interaction, how students greet teachers, visitors to the school, and each other.
- Such behaviors will create an environment that will encourage high academic results.
- When school personnel celebrate those students that have appropriate behavior, it sends the message that the staff appreciates and recognizes when students are extending the effort to use appropriate behaviors.
- When the school personnel fail to purposefully recognize and honor achieving students, then the trouble-makers gain validation.

## What Teachers Can Do to Partner With Parents to Invigorate Parallel Supervision:

- To improve the climate within schools, it must be made clear to everyone that academics come first.
- Staff members must make sure that the adults in the student's family and community members realize that school personnel expect that students will be sent to school to learn and that the adults in the student's family and community will support the school in this demand.
- The adults in the student's family and community members can take pride in the fact that academic discipline will be a major focus within the school and every student will be required to give their best academic effort.
- In schools with the best supervision, administrators let everyone know that they will stay the course when these academic expectations are challenged.

## How Adults in the Families that Have School Age Children and Students Can Work with Educators to Implement Parallel Supervision:

Primary care givers should make sure that the children:

- Show appreciation for the staff members at school who go the "extra mile" to help students that give effective effort and take responsibility so that they can reach their fullest potential.
- Reject being self-centered and self-indulgent and realize that neither school nor society will freely provide for them, to pluck whenever they choose, respect, rewards, and resources without being responsible or being held accountable.
- Place emphasis on moving from a culture of defiance to one of cooperation.
- Understand that in schools with high failure, defiance is often enabled by non-engaging attitudes of the staff; and that parents will support educators who engage the children.
- Realize that there is a price to pay for defiance, while those who comply will be held in high regard.

## How Students Can Cooperate with Peers to Comply with Parallel Supervision:

- Students that attend schools known for academic success usually put more energy into celebrating peers that do the right things, get good grades, and practice good school citizenship.
- Students that attend schools known for academic problems and high failure rates do the opposite; the staff and students regularly put their time and energy into acquiescing and kowtowing to students that are practicing behaviors that will lead to failure.

## How Students Can Partner with the Adults in their Families to Meet the Expectations of Parallel Supervision:

- Adult caregivers and students should work together toward academic development, parents should demand effective effort from their students, and students must strive to do their best in every subject at school.
- Adults in families that have high achieving students insist that their youngsters follow the school rules and guidelines when attending school or school events.

## Four Steps to Student Success (Students, you are in control of your own success)

1. **Be responsible and reliable**
   - Don't follow the loud obnoxious crowd heading for failure
   - Arrive on time and arrive prepared
   - Work thoroughly and smart, listen, learn, and give something extra

2. **Carry yourself in a dignified manner**
   - Don't feed the stereotypes
   - Be clean and neat and maintain consistency of purpose
   - Master and demonstrate a demeanor and decorum that is highly regarded in the mainstream environment

3. **Treat everyone with dignity and respect**
   - Don't base your behavior on how others act
   - Demonstrate a cooperative and collaborative spirit
   - Honor, defend, and support what is good and right

4. **Help someone younger be better**
   - Don't be a bully in word, attitude, or deed
   - Be a positive role model
   - Be a positive mentor for a younger person

# HOW TO IMPLEMENT FOUR-STEP PROCESS OF PARALLEL SUPERVISION

To implement parallel supervision, core curriculum and triangular looping teams of teachers could encourage families, by way of letters, telephone conversation, and conferences to create a set of rules and guidelines in their homes that promote attitudes that are compatible to what the school will expect of students.

The four-step process of parallel supervision gives a student direction and guidance and it provides structure so that students and parents know what is expected. Educators and families become stronger partners when they agree to embrace the four components of parallel supervision:

## 1. Set behavior boundaries and high academic expectations

The operational collectives within individual schools across school districts and at the district level could collaborate to create systems of supervision that would be general guidelines for the individual schools as a whole and for the entire district. These guidelines developed by the operational collectives should cover each of the four components of parallel supervision. The comprehensive guidelines designed by the operational collectives could be a beacon used by core curriculum and triangular looping teams as they design parallel supervision strategies tailored for their situation.

Core curriculum and triangular looping teams of teachers could collaborate to decide how they would design their unique applications of supervision for students while staying within the guidelines of the four components of parallel supervision. Each team should set three to five behavioral boundaries as the guiding principles for students. Each team could communicate to those within the Learning Triad what the team expects behaviorally. The core curriculum and triangular looping teams of teachers could further use the systems designed by the operational collectives as guideposts for the development of systems designed by teams in individual school buildings.

90

When core curriculum and triangular looping teams of teachers express their support for parents in supervision of their children at home and validate the parents' desire for their children to get a good education, it sets the stage for bonds of trust. Bonds of trust between families and the school make it less difficult for families and community members to understand and appreciate that certain behaviors will not be tolerated at school.

When families and educators demonstrate to students that there is an alliance between the adults, it clears a path for student learning.

| Bonds of trust bring support of school rules and guidelines |
| --- |

Bonds of trust bring support of school rules and guidelines and helps families and the community form a tight coalition with educators. Operational collectives and core curriculum and triangular looping teams could insist that students adhere to rules of common civility, good manners, empathy, social justice, fairness, and respect and compassion for others. Each core curriculum and triangular looping team would be expected to be unique and develop individual team rules.

Core curriculum and triangular looping teams could set high academic expectations where students understand that academic achievement is required. Teacher teams could create an atmosphere at school where academic achievement is the central focus and students are required to strive for B's or better and give their best, consistent, and most effective effort on state and national tests.

When advising parents at conferences and in conversations, teacher teams could suggest that parents require students to study school work at home at least 90 minutes each night, five nights a week. Teams of teachers could give students opportunities for input as to what time will be the best time for them to study each evening. Teacher teams might further suggest that families insist upon no television, no surfing the net, no telephone calls, and no visitors during study time. If a student fails to study for a full 90 minutes one or more of the evenings, parents could require their child to make up double the time missed over the weekend.

## 2. Support and monitor students both behaviorally and academically

Once operational collectives and core curriculum and triangular looping teams set behavior boundaries and high academic expectations, the next step would be to **create systems for monitoring and supporting students.** Teacher teams could put systems in place that monitor students and provide support for their success. Many students that are not meeting behavioral or academic expectations like to remain anonymous so that they can escape accountability. They also like to create division between the adults at home and the adults at school. For the good of the students this cannot be allowed.

### Find the Boll Weevils

In Greek mythology Pandora opened the box and pestilence escaped into the world. Analogously, the Boll Weevil is an insect of the beetle family about a quarter of an inch long and lives on cotton plants. The Boll Weevil causes over 100 million dollars of damage to cotton crops each year. The insect bites into the blossom buds of the plant and destroys the flower. It also lays its eggs in some of the holes that it makes and the eggs hatch into small white wormlike creatures called Grubs, which feed on the plant as well. It is very difficult to kill the Grubs and Boll Weevils without destroying the cotton plant.

An extrapolation of the flower and weeds metaphor can bring clarity in reference to understanding one of the roots of problems in schools. Some low-performing, poorly behaving students are Boll Weevils in that they burrow their way into the very fabric of the regular student body—the flowers. Once embedded, the Boll Weevils become anonymous. It is sometimes difficult for the adults at school to identify and apply interventions to help Boll Weevils learn to become successful without alienating the flowers.

A way to identify and isolate the **Boll Weevil students** is to collect grade-related data. Students that make failing grades are usually the same ones that cause most of the attendance and behavior problems at school. Usually, the more failing grades students make, the more problems with behavior and attendance those students have. In a six-period day, students that earn six failing grades will usually be discovered to have serious problems inside and outside of school. The further students move away from six failing grades, the fewer problems they have in school and outside of school.

For instance, students with three failing grades out of six are usually in less trouble than students that have more than three failing grades. Students that have less than three failing grades, although they may have serious problems, are in less trouble than students that have more failing grades.

**There is no research that suggests that large numbers of students consistently receiving failing grades will at some point magically turn themselves around and gain success within Green Culture.** However, when educators discover and identify Boll Weevil students, it is a huge step in establishing an effective monitoring system. Boll Weevil students, once identified, should be supported without delay. Interventions can be introduced to help Boll Weevil students learn to focus and compel them to give effective effort when pursuing academics.

Boll Weevils exist not only among students but among administrators, teachers, and parents as well. **Boll Weevil administrators** most often were given positions through the "good ol' boy network." They are sometimes good at the delivery of current education rhetoric. However, they are not so good at delivering courageous education leadership that advocates a school culture of order, unity, and quality. **Boll Weevil teachers** usually have little interest in student learning; they are self-centered rather than student-centered; they are often an embarrassment to good teachers and an annoyance to the teachers union. **Boll Weevil parents** spend less time mentoring and monitoring their children and more time chasing the intoxicants of life.

Core curriculum and triangular looping teams could set specific criteria for identifying Boll Weevils. Students would be monitored to discover if they are complying with behavioral and academic expectations. Operational collectives and cross categorical core curriculum and triangular looping teams could find ways to monitor the academic effort of students so that students would know that educators will tolerate nothing less than effective effort. Teacher teams could create conditions that support the achievement of good grades and learning at the highest levels.

School leaders could move more quickly toward better schools when they desist from allowing Boll Weevils to determine the culture, climate, and direction of the schools. Often times school leaders invest too much time, energy, and money into the appeasement of Boll

Weevils. Education leaders can more effectively help improve schools when the emphasis is on the achievers and those that give effective effort rather than the Boll Weevils.

## 3. Relentlessly level consequences to challengers

Operational collectives and core curriculum and triangular looping teams could develop **systems of multiple escalating consequences** at school for those students that step outside of the behavioral boundaries or do not strive to meet the academic expectations of the school or district.

Teacher teams could suggest to parents that it would help create a powerful learning environment **when students realize that they will have to face consequences at school and at home if expectations are not met.** Operational collectives could establish discipline system designs that contain due process, sequence, escalating consequences, a trail of communication, and multiple levels.

Educators could agree not to allow the discipline system to be driven by emotion or anger. A main ingredient in establishing trust between educators, students, families, and community members is the perception that the system is fair. When a discipline system has design, it maintains the integrity of fairness. When a system is perceived unfair it is difficult for that system to gain trust and support.

Teacher teams could create discipline systems that have sequence, are organized, and present a progression for educators to follow and a "no surprises" process that parents and students can easily understand. The sequence would include definite procedures that would occur each time students are placed in the discipline system by educators. The sequence would be predictable so that students and parents realize what happens at each stage of the process.

**Students, by law, must be accorded due process.** The due process portion of the discipline system design is a wonderful place to interject a lesson for the students so that the discipline system could be used as a learning experience.

Operational collectives could set up a check and balance system where staff members are required to give students the opportunity to tell experiences from their points of view. Within due process, administrators might also use an effective process:

1. In a private meeting, ask the student what happened.
2. In a meeting with the others involved, allow everyone the opportunity to say what happened from a personal view. Useful rules to use in this portion of due process are:
   - The participants can only speak to the administrator.
   - Only the adults in the room may ask questions about the incident.
   - Only one person may speak at a time.
3. Allow each person involved to have a chance at rebuttal.
4. Ask each person what percentage of the fault they own.
5. Ask each person what they could have done differently to make the situation less volatile.
6. Present the students with a positive, alternate way to have handled the situation.

**Creating a discipline system design:**

- Teams of teachers should communicate to parents and students the details of the discipline system design and that repeated violation of the discipline codes will bring escalating consequences.
- Penalties that begin with minimal consequences would incrementally increase in intensity. Students and parents would understand that if students continuously violate the discipline code, further methods would be used in an attempt to adjust the student's attitude toward compliance.
- Teams of teachers should create systems and strategies for communicating to families each time consequences are leveled.
- A good strategy is to communicate to staff members that initiate referrals concerning the consequences leveled to the student.
- This trail of communication would keep everyone involved informed of the situation.

To address the needs of students that do not seem to get the message and repeatedly violate the discipline system, an extended level of discipline could be initiated. There could be a definite point of termination where students that insist upon being perpetrators would no longer be accepted in the regular discipline system. Students that are deliberate nuisances have to understand that they must either get serious about getting an education or realize that they will be excluded from participation in school related activities including attending school.

Suspension is of course a last resort but everyone in the Learning Triad needs to understand that suspension will be implemented when behavior is inappropriately severe or repeating. Students that have experienced the discipline system a number of times and continue to demonstrate inappropriate behavior obviously need other strategies to be implemented.

Every effort could be made to involve, invite, and include adult caregivers, especially the adult caregivers of American-black students, in the education of their children. Educators in top schools assume that adult caregivers love their children and adult caregivers of American-black students could certainly be included in that assumption. Most adult caregivers want the best for their children, and it is important that educators convince adult caregivers that the acquisition of a solid education is the best way for youngsters to gain a high quality of life. When students are not required to practice appropriate behavior and stay within boundaries, they are being set-up to have a difficult life.

The teacher teams that agree to confront every transgression by students create a consistency that gives energy to connections of trust. Staff members, students, and parents feel safe when they realize that policies, guidelines, and rules are relentlessly enforced at school. The teams that decide to eliminate excessive warnings and decree that one warning is enough, escalate penalties for repeat perpetrators, and send the message that the adults in the school are in charge, might find a decline in defiant transgressions. Teacher teams can agree that student challengers will be dealt with sternly, immediately, and fairly, but with a lesson-to-be-learned attitude, and each situation will be individually decided. Finally, operational collectives and cross categorical core curriculum and triangular looping teams could give attention to team requirements for school attendance and commitment to require punctuality to class.

# Example of a Discipline System and What Educators Should Do:

1. *Verbally reprimand a student (One warning per semester).*

2. *Create and use the Redirect Center to remove challengers for a short time. (The Redirect Center is a monitored quiet area for study where students may be sent when they are tardy to class or disruptive in class; the rules within the center should be strict and in most situations students may report to the next period class at the changing of classes.)*
   a. Upon the fourth time sent to the Redirect Center within a semester, the student should be given a letter, and the parent should be sent a copy of the letter that warns of termination of the regular redirect sequence.
   b. The fifth assignment to the Redirect Center carries with it the additional penalty of an after-school detention; or referral to administration for being ejected from in-school suspension (ISS) if waiting for suspension.
   c. A challenger could be sent to the Redirect Center after being suspended to wait for school to end so that he or she can ride home on the bus or walk home. (If the challenger is ejected from the Redirect Center a day of suspension should be added.)
   d. Tenth time in Redirect Center, student is assigned ISS for the next day.

3. *Assign challengers to after-school-detention (ASD) for some rule infractions.*
   a. On the ninth assignment to ASD, challengers should be given a letter, and the parent should be sent a copy of the letter that warns of termination of the regular ASD sequence
   b. On the tenth and subsequent assignments to ASD, challengers should be also assigned to ISS.
   c. If a challenger fails to attend or gets ejected from ASD, he or she should be assigned to ISS for the next day

4. *Send some challengers to in-school suspension (ISS).*
   a. Challengers assigned to ISS must consider the following procedure:
      • Once assigned to ISS but removed because of a rule infraction, the challenger will receive a one-day suspension and return to ISS upon return to school. (Students must complete day in ISS.)
      • Student has one avenue of reprieve from returning to ISS—if challenger's parent will accompany him or her to school for a conference after the suspension.
      • If the challenger leaves immediately by way of pick-up by an adult family member or permission to walk home from an adult family member, that day will count as the day of suspension and the challenger may return the next day; or the challenger must finish the day in the Redirect Center and serve the suspension the next day.

b. If a challenger is assigned for a tenth time to ISS within a semester, a letter that warns of termination of sequence should be given to the challenger and mailed to the parent explaining that upon the next and subsequent assignments to ISS, challengers will:
   - No longer be received in ISS, but will be suspended in escalating sequence instead.

c. Upon eleventh time assigned to ISS, one day of suspension is assigned and the student may return to class.
   - Twelve times in ISS gets two days of suspension and escalating days of suspension subsequently.
   - Challengers may return to class after the suspensions.

5. *Level out-of-school suspension to some challengers.*
   a. Upon first suspension the parent is asked to return with challenger for conference before student's return.
   b. If parent does not return with the challenger, make note of this.
   c. On fourth time suspended (number of times, not days), give a letter to warn of termination of sequence to challenger and send a copy of the letter to the challenger's parent.
   d. On fifth time suspended and subsequently, challenger should receive a 10-day out-of-school suspensions.
   e. On the third 10-day suspension, recommend to superintendent for expulsion for 90 days (The challenger is a continuous nuisance.)

6. *Recommend expulsion for 90 days after third 10-day suspension or second fight.*

7. *Recommend expulsion for 180 days after the selling of drugs, possession of weapons, third fight, or striking a teacher.*

# 4. Consistently give students praise and rewards for compliance

Operational collectives and cross categorical core curriculum and triangular looping teams could develop systems for granting students on the success end of the academic spectrum praise, attention, and rewards. In one way this motivates the achievers to continue achieving and motivates the Boll Weevil students to move toward becoming successful so that some of the rewards, compliments, and accolades will go to them.

When students meet the expectations, responsible adults at the students' homes and educators could praise them, recognize their success, and reward them. The school atmosphere could be saturated with praise; staff members could capitalize on every opportunity to say something good about students who are compliant with the QUO Process

Private or quiet praise is terrific, but public praise where groups of students can hear the praise and the reason for the praise is even more effective. Staff members should not be

> Private or quiet praise is terrific, but public praise where groups of students can hear the praise and the reason for the praise is even more effective.

reluctant to have a pizza party or some other form of reward for groups of students that have done something outstanding. Praise is also another way to send the message about what kinds of behaviors are expected within different venues. Students need to realize that although the staff is strict and unwavering, they do it because they care.

**It is important that educators do not give rewards or attention to students that are undeserving.** Students that do not comply with the boundaries set or the expectations stated would find it extremely difficult to gain accolades and praise in a good school. Such students would be denied participation in activities and events at good schools.

# IMPROVE CULTURE AND CLIMATE AT SCHOOL

The most difficult element to achieve in protecting the learning environment is improving the culture and climate. The culture of a school is, "How things are done at the school." The climate of a school is, "The prevailing attitude." Many educators in schools that are experiencing academic low achievement often avoid addressing discipline issues and have allowed students in such schools to run amuck. When teacher teams place heavy emphasis on improving culture and climate, the school's atmosphere can be transformed from one of low achievement to one of success.

Good schools are places where academics are the priority. Educators within schools that are dedicated to improving the school's culture and climate must agree that they will relentlessly confront defiance and inappropriateness. Students must be guided to understand that an atmosphere of high expectations will be nurtured where the adults in the school not only believe that the students can and will be successful but that staff members will accept nothing less. The message should be sent to the adults in families that have children of school age and to the community that not only will defiance and inappropriateness not be tolerated, but students will also be required to give effective effort in every class, every day.

To move toward improved culture and climate, it is important for the school to encourage strong values and require that students emulate what is appropriate. Educators in great schools require students to treat staff members with respect and dignity. In the most effective schools the work ethic and personal responsibility of students are held in the highest regard while punctuality and regular attendance are priorities. In an ideal school, every teacher in every class has the highest academic expectations for their students.

Another way to improve the culture and climate at school is for the adults in the Learning Triad to insist upon the practice of **Ubiquitous Civility**. Everyone in the Learning Triad should practice civility at all times while at school or attending school functions. Students must learn the difference between school behavior and behavior better received in a different venue. Students need to understand that different kinds of language should be used in different places, and they must make good choices about when and where to use which kind of language. Without judging inappropriate-school language as inherently bad, educators must require students to use only appropriate-school language at school.

Highly effective schools initiate a culture of order by introducing a **Philosophy of Success**. In such schools staff members make certain that students know that teachers and administrators will relentlessly encourage the practice of behaviors that will lead to success, while confronting the practice of behaviors that will lead to failure. Educators in great schools expect colleagues to make sure that students understand that the adults are the leaders and the authorities at the school. Several strategies should be implemented within a school to demonstrate that educators are doing their part in establishing parallel supervision.

Culture and climate inside a school may most strongly influence an educator's ability to protect the learning environment. Students are more likely to meet expectations when they are clearly explained by educators and students know that consequences quickly follow inappropriate student behavior relentlessly every time it occurs.

Students and parents must trust that objectivity always rules an educator in disciplinary situations. Educators must remember that when they assign inappropriate consequences to a student other students and parents see this as evidence of inequity. When inequity exists, the integrity of the entire system comes under question and some will use this as license for noncompliance.

# PRESENT EDUCATORS AS POSITIVE AND GENUINE ROLE MODELS

Administrators in quality schools hire quality staff members at every level, many of whom are American-blacks. In top schools all staff members including American-blacks are celebrated for their personal accomplishments. In top schools staff members are presented to the students as role models for student academic development. Students need to have several American-black adults that have successfully negotiated Green Culture that they can see and hold in high regard, and people on the school staff are wonderful candidates for that purpose.

The same line of thinking could follow in schools when it comes to hiring, promoting, and presenting American-black staff members as role models to the students. Deserving American-whites have long been presented as role models for American-black children, but American-white youngsters need to see deserving American-black professionals and especially school staff members as heroes and positive role models as well.

**Being presented as a positive role model brings with it responsibility.** Therefore, it is imperative that educators working with American students are willing to provide role modeling, mentoring, and monitoring. In the past, such modeling occurred at home from adult caretakers before the student ever arrived at school; in many cases that is no longer true of the homes today. "It is not fair for us to have to do this" is the cry that might ring from the voices of some educators across America when they are asked to be heroes and role-models for students. Nevertheless, educators must attempt to save students from a life of ignorance; they must strive to help students become productive participants in America's capitalistic democratic republic.

## Educator Diligence

Students that repeatedly choose negative behaviors when identified could be confronted with creative interventions to help as many as possible escape a malignant co-dependency on social, economic, spiritual, and intellectual welfare. The result of educator diligence in the greater society is that the American taxpayers are going to be freed from being strapped with the burden of taking care of an uneducated, unsophisticated, powerless ineffectual group of people.

# STRUCTURE FEELS SAFE AND SECURE

Youngsters need and want structure. They want to feel safe and they want consistency in their lives so that they can feel secure. Young people want pride in their parents and pride in their school. They want to know that the adults in their lives care about them. Young people want to be able to depend on adults to keep the best interest of youngsters at the forefront.

## Examples of Ways to Create Structure

### Institute a consistent consequence progression:
- Students must understand that when they choose inappropriate behaviors consequences will follow.
- In effective schools when students repeat inappropriateness, the consequences increase in severity.
- Staff members in top schools impress upon the students that the adults are in charge of the school and will tolerate nothing short of compliance to school rules and guidelines.
- Within parallel supervision, staff members strongly encourage parents to implement the same attitude and philosophy at home.

### Reclaim classroom and hallway etiquette:
- The atmosphere in the hallways sends a clear message as to the expectations of the school.
- When the noise level in the halls is too high, students are chasing each other, large groups of students are standing, blocking the flow of traffic, teachers are not standing outside their doors during passing periods, and there is student traffic and noise during class time, these are indicators that the hallways at the school are out of control.
- In the best case scenario, students are encouraged to use "12-inch voices" when they are engaged in personal conversations. (The volume of voice is so low that no one further away than 12 inches is able to determine what is being said.) This would be expected in the hallways, in the cafeteria, and in classrooms.

### Teachers assign detention:
- In good schools the administration empowers teachers to assign detentions for inappropriate behavior or for failure to complete and turn in academic assignments.
- Students need evidence that teachers will be relentless in confronting both. Consequences need to be swift, fair, and just.

**Create a Redirect Center:**

- Within the newly created school culture, promptness, regular attendance, punctuality, effective effort, and appropriate classroom behavior hold high priority.
- Educators in great schools establish the idea that non-compliance in any areas of the school is unacceptable.
- In collaborative schools, students that arrive to class after the tardy bell would not be accepted in the classroom.
- Students that are inappropriate in class would be either given a referral to the administrator by the teacher or sent to the redirect center for the remainder of the period.
- At the departure bell, the redirect center monitor should release the students so that the students may move to the next assigned area or class.
- One student should not be allowed to interrupt the learning of others.

Employers complain that the two main reasons that workers get fired are that they have an attendance or punctuality problem or that they cannot get along with fellow workers. According to recent reports from the business community, young American-black workers are experiencing problems with attendance, punctuality, and cooperation with workers more than most. Schools must provide opportunities for students to practice skills that will help them be successful in the job market.

To support that goal, the redirect center monitor should assign the student a five-paragraph essay to write during his or her stay in the center; the essay should discuss one of the following topics:

- First time assigned (Why is it important to be punctual to class?)
- Second time assigned (Three strategies I will use never to be tardy again.)
- Third time assigned (Why is being placed in the discipline system detrimental to learning?)
- Fourth time assigned (Assigned an after-school detention.)
- Fifth or more assignments (Assigned two after-school detentions)

**The redirect center monitor should inform the student that:**

- He or she should write his or her name and the name of the teacher of the missed class on the essay.
- Each paper will be checked to make certain that it complies to the rubric design.
- Papers collected that comply to the rubric design will be handed in to the appropriate teacher so that the student can get some percentage of credit for class that day.
- If he or she does not complete the assignment, an after-school detention will be scheduled.

**At the end of the school day, the redirect center monitor should:**

- Turn the list of students for each grade into administration secretaries for record keeping.

- Place the collected essays written by the students into the mailboxes of the appropriate teachers.
- Turn in the list of students assigned to after-school detention to the appropriate person.

A teacher that receives an essay written by a student that failed to attend class because he or she was detained in the redirect center should grade the essay. (The student should be required to re-write and hand in by the next class meeting the essay that was not well constructed. If the student fails to comply, assign the student to detention.) When the student's essay is acceptable, give the student half credit or more for the period of class missed.

### Launch daily hall sweeps:
- It should be mandatory that students have hall passes when they are traveling during class time.
- Students should know that if they are discovered in the hall without a pass they will be escorted to the in-school suspension room where they will be required to study for the remainder of the day.

### Establish monitored lunch:
- In most public schools the lunch period is one of the most behavior-sensitive times of the student's day; it is the one time when large numbers of students are congregated in an assigned place with unstructured time.
- The schools where high percentages of students are scoring at the lowest levels on state and national tests are also the schools where there are more behavior problems; such schools should have monitored lunch periods.
- Introducing monitored lunch is for the safety of the students and the protection of the learning environment.
- Staff members and administrators must show high visibility and consistently interact with the students during the lunch period.

# Chapter 10
# Introduce Order by Improving Communication

*"In order to successfully implement a change process within a system a "critical mass" of people must be developed by using the three Cs: communication, collaboration and culture. The change process will stall unless sufficient attention is given to communication. Creating a collaborative environment has been described as the single most important factor for successful school improvement and should be the first order of business for those seeking to improve their schools."*

Rick Dufore, *Professional Learning Communities*

### *"I Didn't Know."*

*"I did not know that my daughter was missing first period everyday. I drop her off on my way to work and I assume that she is going to her classes."* Mrs. Morris paused and looked down at her hands that were folded in her lap; I sensed that she was experiencing an explosion of feelings.

She moved the attendance letter closer as if she was trying to read something written between the lines but, invisible to the naked eye. She continued, *"It says here that Noshiba has missed 15 days in her first period class; I just can't believe it. And what is it with these grades? These are the most horrible grades that she has ever received."*

Suddenly her caution turned to anger, as she said, *"Why haven't I been contacted about this? How do you expect parents to help the school and intervene with our children when a person gets this kind of report with only two weeks remaining in the quarter?"*

Mrs. Morris was what I refer to in my own thinking as a "walk-on," someone arriving to speak to an administrator without an appointment. I generally take about 10 to 30 of these kinds of interactions weekly. There is no time to prepare, collect thoughts, or to gather information in preparation for the meeting. I said, *"Mrs. Morris, let me apologize; it is our intent to communicate information to parents regularly."*

She would not let me off the hook; she said, *"Regularly?"* She held up a letter with the school letterhead in plain view and continued, *"This is the only communication about this issue that I have received from the school. With less than two weeks in the quarter what can I do to turn this around? According to what I see on this progress report, I need to talk with the three teachers that Nosheba received the three Fs from; I want to give them a piece of my mind. There is no way that my baby should be receiving anybody's F."*

I relaxed for a moment before I tried to answer. I knew that Mrs. Morris' belief about sending progress reports early was compatible with mine and I always struggled when parents arrived complaining that their child received one or more Fs but no timely communication had occurred from school to home.

I knew that I was in an indefensible position concerning the progress report issue. I felt awful; I realized that in the eyes of this parent the school had dropped the ball. I also realized that from a teacher union point of view suggesting that teachers begin sending progress reports earlier or sending progress reports, both positive reports and failure reports, to more students might not be well received. As an administrator, I was between a rock and a hard place; the progress report issue would have to be confronted again with the teachers but it was merely part of a much larger communication issue.

Perhaps Noshiba Morris and her mother could have benefitted from earlier and more frequent communication from teachers about academic progress but that is just a small piece of a larger concern for schools. The greater issue is that educators have an obligation within schools and classrooms to create order by protecting the learning environment.

The implementation of the QUO Process requires that collaborative cooperatives and operational collectives form to first determine if improvements surrounding lines of communication at school or within the district should be considered or reviewed, then teacher teams could plan how improved communication can be established.

Lines of communication may be established to keep everyone in the Learning Triad in the know. Former first lady and now Senator Hilary Clinton in her book, *It Takes A Village*, advocated the idea that it takes collaboration to educate even a single child. But, in order to be certain that what the child is taught at school is congruent, teachers can meet to determine which information is important to know. Consequently, communication between all of the stakeholders is of utmost importance.

Core curriculum and triangular looping teams of teachers could collaboratively form systems of communication that would be designed to keep everyone informed concerning the business of the team and the progress of the students that the team serves. Core curriculum and triangular looping teams of teachers could set up meetings where adults and educators in a school community could attempt to reach consensus concerning what atmosphere and general practices they would like to see at school. Teacher teams could also initiate purposeful dialog with students to make certain that students have a forum for concerns and that students understand expectation. Each team could determine ways to regularly communicate with other teams and to have ongoing interaction with levels looping cooperatives to insure vertical articulation. Conversations between educators at individual schools could help determine at what grade level and intensity the content and sequence of information would be taught to students.

Both internal and external communication strategies could be employed to make certain that everyone is represented and the concerns of all can be heard. The atmosphere and general practices of the school could be made clear to everyone, both inside the school and within the community. In this way the opinions of every stakeholder would be valued, seen as important, and held in high regard by the school leadership. Objectives and goals that are specific, measurable, achievable, results-oriented, and time-bound is not enough; they would be best received if they are well communicated and agreed upon.

## Communication's Main Goal

The major goal of improved communication is to provide avenues of input for all of the stakeholders. When more avenues exist that facilitate the collaboration of a wider cadre of people from different groups to speak to each other, it is evidence that the avenues of communication have been expanded. Further evidence that communication is better at a school is when there is improved participation in school activities by parents, students, and staff. Several strategies could be implemented by those within the Learning Triad to guarantee and speed an improvement in communication. Each group within the Learning Triad has a responsibility to improve communication. Every effort made in this regard is to help students reach their full potential.

To implement the communication component, at least one strategy in each of the areas of QUO Process should be initiated the first year and others could be added in successive years. For instance, along with finding ways to protect the learning environment, teams of teachers could communicate concerning how to create systematic learning cycles *or* how to manage direct data. One component of each area of the QUO Process could be discussed and implemented yearly. Some of the components might take more than one year to develop; nevertheless, a progression of development could be planned that would expand communication throughout the school, the district, and the community.

Core curriculum and triangular looping teams of teachers could decide to initiate the strategy of collaborating to create common assessments in the area of improving communication with administrators and colleagues. One or more teams might also decide to initiate the strategy of reviewing grades with students once a week in the area of improving communication with students. A team might decide to initiate the strategy of making night calls once a week in the area of improving communication with parents. However, once a team decides on an approach, everyone on the team must use the agreed upon techniques.

# WAYS TO DEVELOP BETTER LINES
# OF COMMUNICATION

## Suggestions for Administrators:

**Hold monthly staff meetings;** however, rather than a series of announcements by the principal, break from the status quo by using such meetings for staff development and school improvement progress. Staff meetings will also:

- Allow faculty members to give presentations on workshops they attended and innovative delivery strategies they have used.
- Clarify or provide input for tweaking currently used initiatives.

**Hold monthly department chairpersons meetings to:**

- Gain input from department chairpersons who are generally held in high regard by members of the faculty and also by people throughout the school district.
- Use the department chairpersons as sounding boards for ideas; they usually have a wealth of corporate history and know where many of the trouble spots may exist.
- Pass along information from the central office and review agendas for staff meetings.

**Hold monthly faculty advisory council meetings to:**

- Speak with about 15 percent of the most influential members of the staff as a forum for open discussion for ideas or concerns of the staff and as another sounding board for the administration.
- Offer an opportunity to a diverse cross section of the staff to give input so that their perspectives are heard.

**Hold regular meetings with academic departments to:**

- Listen to department concerns and to review expectations for the department; meet on a rotating basis twice a month.
- Allow each department such as math, science, communication arts, then social studies to meet on a rotating basis.
- Offer staff members who will not share ideas in a large meeting an opportunity to be more communicative in a smaller setting with more familiar individuals such as friends in the department.
- Create an atmosphere where department members can give interesting insights on how different initiatives impact individual departments.
- Give the members of departments an opportunity to be instrumental in helping make a plan successful.

**Hold monthly meetings with various support staff members so that:**

- Secretaries, cafeteria workers, custodians, security personnel, and the school nurse play a role in the overall operation of school
  a. *Secretaries keep everyone in the school connected.*
  b. *Secretaries are often the first and last people that visitors see or that people speak with when people visit or telephone someone in the building.*
  c. *Secretaries often give people a first impression about the school; therefore it is important that they understand the message that the administration is trying to send so that they can express that message as they interact with people.*

- The input of cafeteria workers is heard
  a. *Cafeteria workers are the only people in the school that come into contact with almost every student in school every day.*
  b. *Since many students now have breakfast at school, the attitude that cafeteria workers have toward students sometimes determines if students will have a great day or a challenging day at school.*

- Custodians and maintenance personnel feel like they are an important part of the team
  a. *Custodians and maintenance personnel can make the building aesthetically pleasing.*
  b. *When custodians and maintenance personnel do a great job, the people that work inside of the building and the students more often have feelings of pride in the school.*
  c. *Administrators should endeavor to uplift custodians and maintenance workers by requiring that students and staff members treat them with respect and dignity.*

- Security team members have an avenue for input
  a. *Security team members are important to the safety of staff members and students.*
  b. *Security team members and the administration must be in sync so that everyone in the school can feel safe.*

- The nurse can have regular opportunities to meet with the principal
  a. *The nurse can be helpful in the school's overall operation.*
  b. *The nurse often has information about students that could help educators better understand individual students so that educators can be more effective.*

The input of people in these categories is valuable and should be heard; many times they will have insights that could help the administration be more effective in the logistical designs that help the school operate smoothly. Including support workers in the decision-making at the school helps them feel buy-in and ownership.

**Hold rotating core curriculum staff development meetings so that:**

- During the school day substitute teachers can relieve departments of core curriculum teachers for staff development and planning.
- The principal and others can work with department members to align curriculum, coordinate courses with the state guidelines, create common assessments, develop assessment-based instruction units, and discuss, share, and practice lesson delivery plans.
- Opportunities for collaborative cooperatives to work together can be achieved.

**Hold quarterly teacher chat meetings to allow:**

- Individual teachers to voluntarily meet with the principal when he or she is on a conference period or lunch break
  a. *Sometimes no matter how many meetings the administration has, some people within the school setting may feel unheard or under-appreciated.*
  b. *The principal should hold these meetings somewhere other than his or her office— perhaps in the teachers' work area or lounge.*

**Codify procedures to:**

- Improve communication among staff members
  a. *The important information should be put in a booklet or in an e-mail attachment that explains processes that will occur regularly throughout the school year.*
  b. *Any staff member should have access to the information for review at will.*

## To Open Lines of Communication for the Students, the Administrators Should Develop the Following:

**Hold monthly meetings with the Student Council to:**

- Empower students so that they have input to the administration.
- Bring the pulse of the student body to a legitimate forum.
- Offer a forum so that achieving students can have conversation with the administration.
- Allow those students that are willing to help make positive change in the school an opportunity to be heard.

**Quarterly grade level meetings to:**

- Set and review expectations at the beginning of each quarter.
- Extend important information peculiar to each grade level.
- Give public praise and attention to deserving students.
- Offer the principal, counselors, administrators, and selected staff members 30 minutes to give motivational remarks to the students.

**Shadow a student once a quarter so that:**

- Each building administrator could accompany students from different social groups and different races—both male and female—to class for a day.

- You can get into the traffic flow between classes and acquire the real flavor of classroom climate.
- Students and teachers could see the humanness of the administration.
- You could witness great teaching throughout the day.
- You could have an opportunity to write notes of appreciation to teachers that have an exceptional lesson that day.

## To Open Lines of Communication For Parents and Community Members, the Administrators Should Do the Following:

### Hold annual stakeholders meeting to:
- Further communicate with parents and community members and to extend the hand of welcome.
- Offer religious and community leaders an opportunity to give input at the beginning of each school year so that they will know what to expect in the upcoming school year.
- Set the tone and cover new guidelines that students and visitors need to know.

### Help parents establish a parent organization so that:
- The parents will have a consistent way to directly support the school and the students.
- The organization could provide input and determine its own direction.
- The organization could produce monthly newsletters to keep parents, students, teachers, and other interested persons informed.

These ideas can be instituted from an administrative level but individual teachers should make improvements in communication in their classrooms. Students usually progress more rapidly when teachers monitor them more closely; teachers can accomplish this by making certain that students know what their grade is weekly, know how many assignments they are missing weekly, and require that over the weekend the assignments are completed and turned in on Monday. It is of vital importance that teachers maintain lines of close communication with their students. Students that are closely monitored experience less failure and learn more.

> **Students that are closely monitored experience less failure and learn more.**

# SUGGESTIONS FOR TEACHERS

## In Communicating with the Administrators and Colleagues, Teachers Could Develop the Following:

### Collaborative teams that:
- Encourage teachers to entertain conversation about the subject they teach with others who teach the same subject for improved instruction.
- Determine the alignment of the curriculum strengths' teaching units.

- Collate state indicators into the appropriate courses for improved organization.
- Decide what should be covered in the courses taught for revitalized instruction.
- Discuss how to help students learn more, and learn faster to increase individual knowledge by sharing.
- Create quarterly common assessments for the courses they teach with incremental measurements to determine student progression
- Collect direct data to determine the level of comprehension of the students and the level of effectiveness of the teacher's individual delivery techniques.

## To Open Lines of Communication with Students,' Teachers Could Do the Following:

**Give and take input from students by:**
- Reviewing grades with each student one day each week.
- Requiring that all work missed be completed and turned in by Monday of the following week.
- Allowing students, through brainstorming, cooperative group discussions, and open-forum class discussion, the opportunity to evaluate units, give opinions of lessons, and suggestions for improvement.

## To Open Lines of Communication with Parents and Community Members, Teachers Could Develop the Following:

**Make weeknight calls to:**
- Improve external communication collectively; teachers should select a night of the week that they will phone the parents of 10 students.
- Phone the parents of six students that are deserving of praise; the parents of two students that are struggling academically, but are currently improving; and the parents of two students that are currently having difficulty, either behaviorally or academically.
- Demonstrate to the community that the staff cares about student success.

**Send graded assignments home so that:**
- Parents can see the quality of their children's work.
- Teachers could give students rewards for having parents write a comment and sign the paper to be returned.
- Parents could see the teacher's written comments to better understand his or her expectations.

**Send progress reports early in the quarter to:**
- Give the parents of struggling students time to intervene and help the students improve in time to make a difference
- Provide the parent information about student progress within the first two weeks of class, especially for students that are struggling.
- Allow parents a chance to motivate and encourage students.

# SUGGESTIONS FOR STUDENTS

## To Open Lines of Communication with Educators, Students Could Do the Following:

### Adopt teacher-pleasing behaviors:
- Arrive to class on time every day.
- Have regular attendance.
- Give undivided attention to the teacher's remarks about the lesson.
- Do your best on every assignment.
- Turn in all assignments on time.
- Aspire to really understand the subject matter.
- Have a friendly demeanor with the teachers.

### Ask for help when you don't understand what is being presented so that you:
- Can have a more complete understanding of what the teachers are attempting to relay.
- Help create a scholarly atmosphere in the class which will encourage other students to become more involved.

### Follow the rules and guidelines of the school and classrooms so that you:
- Avoid detention and suspensions, therefore creating a better chance of making good grades.
- Do not miss classes because of having to face consequences for inappropriate behavior.
- Do not have to experience the unpleasantness of punishments, and consequences for violating school rules that in the long run will negatively impact learning.

## To Open Lines of Communication with Peers, Students Could Develop the Following:

### Join more than one learning team so that you:
- Have a support group for learning in the core curriculum.
- Gain a more comprehensive understanding of the information.
- Team with students from the classes of several teachers to help each other learn.
- Meet regularly to study together.

### Help another student learn what you know so that you:
- Learn more about the subject when you teach another student.
- Learn from the student that you teach to increase your understanding of the subject.
- Help someone else improve their understanding of the subject.

**Express to other students that you are not to be interrupted when you are doing homework so that you:**
- Make it less difficult to honor your pre-arranged study time during the week, an hour and a half each day Sunday through Thursday.
- Alert your friends so that they can agree not to interrupt.
- Inspire your friends; you might even arrange to study on the same schedule so that all of you will be available for other activities at the same time.

## To Open Lines Of Communication with Parents, Students Could Develop the Following:

**Spread the news about great teachers so that parents know about:**
- Favorite teachers and can find ways to support them.
- The great things that are happening in school.
- Issues so that they have information on which to base their votes in elections concerning school-related issues.

**Invite parents to school on special occasions so that they:**
- Can participate in important or fun activities that occur.
- Remember to attend parent teacher conference and open houses.
- Can support significant athletic, awards, performance, and college night events.
- Can bring their friends to school events to help spread school pride.

**Talk to parents about academics and aspirations so that they can:**
- Provide support for the student's success.
- Make sure that the student is on the correct path to achieve goals.

# SUGGESTIONS FOR ADULTS IN A STUDENT'S FAMILY

## To Open Lines of Communication with the Educators, Adults in a Student's Family Could Do the Following:

**Introduce yourselves to school administrators so you will:**
- Know administrators personally.
- Feel comfortable interacting with the school leaders.
- Demonstrate to the students that educators and adult family members are in accord.

**Phone administrators when you have a question about school so they can:**
- Discover the truth about rumors.
- Be cautious and ask questions about a student's interpretation about what occurred at school; sometimes a student's view is distorted. You can then hear insights of administrators about occurrences at school before reaching final conclusions.

**Touch base with the student's teachers at least twice a month so that:**
* The youngster's academics could be more closely monitored.
* Teachers know that your family cares about the student's academic success.
* Working together between the family and teachers is easier.

## To Open Lines of Communication with Students, Parents Could Develop the Following:

**Review the student handbook with the student to:**
* Make sure that the student understands the rules and guidelines of the school.
* Be certain that students and adults in your family understand what is expected at school.
* Be sure that students realize the consequences for non-compliance to rules.
* Make sure that the students understand that your family knows and supports the rules so that the student is less likely to become a challenger.

**Demonstrate to the student that you support the school by:**
* Demonstrating support for the school and educators therein.
* Attending a few of the school functions each year.
* Pursuing civil and cordial contact with educators.

**Be proactive in asking the students about school every day so that:**
* They understand that you care about education
* The education priority is reinforced daily
* They see that you care about what is happening in the student's life

## To Open Lines of Positive Communication with Other Adults About the Schools, Adults in a Student's Family Could Develop the Following:

**A positive dialog about the schools with other adults by:**
* Organizing, booster clubs, and other groupings that support the school.
* Writing letters to the editor of the local news about good educators.
* Finding ways to publicize the good that is happening in the schools.
* Working in the community to gain support for quality personnel, materials and supplies.
* Persuading businesses in the community to take an active interest in the schools to help schools keep the facilities, technology, and supplies replenished and up-to-date.

Students who have adult family members that are active in school-related clubs and participate in school-related activities usually have good grades and attendance. Also, schools usually reflect and often create a reputation for the community. For instance, what people think of the school is also what they think of the community; this thinking could also reflect either negatively or positively concerning the value of property; therefore adults in a student's family should strive to make the reputation of the school a good one. When adults in the families of students inside a community show an interest in the schools, it demonstrates to others that children within the community are viewed as important. **The quality of the school is in direct correlation to the amount and quality of parental involvement**

It is the responsibility of individual educators to facilitate positive communication between all groups so that it is the best that it can be. When core curriculum and triangular looping team teachers combine improved communication with parallel supervision, the school environment becomes fertile for learning and paves the way for unity and the creation of systemic learning cycles.

# Part Five
# To Develop Unity, Implement a Systemic Learning Cycle

- Authenticate the curriculum

- Implement Assessment-Based Instruction (ABI)

# Chapter 11
# Authenticate the Curriculum

*"Each department should use the district's curriculum goals, standards and benchmarks to identify the general goal for the course or grade level they are teaching. The teams of teachers responsible for teaching a particular course or grade level should identify the essential student outcomes for each course or grade level. Teaching teams should write common course or grade-level descriptions and distribute them to students; these should include the general goals of the course, the essential outcomes students should achieve, and the means by which student achievement will be assessed. The team should develop common comprehensive assessment strategies that will produce academic data on the teacher's students both individually and collectively as a class. The team should identify the proficiency level that all students should achieve, review results of the collective student achievement, identify problem areas, and develop plans to address areas of failure."*

Rick Dufore, *Professional Learning Communities*

If teachers teach and students learn the "right stuff," academic performance of students on standardized assessments will improve. Collaborative cooperatives, elementary teachers that teach the same grade level, and secondary teachers that teach in the same core curriculum subject area, should meet to authenticate the curriculum.

## The Curriculum Authentication Process (A three- to five-year endeavor)

Collaborative cooperatives should:
1. Review the state descriptors and practice ACT or SAT tests from computer Internet systems to discover what students need to know to score well on the standardized tests.
2. Inventory course offerings and match state descriptors and national test

117

information to course offerings (Make sure that the course offerings sequence is appropriate).

3. Decide if all courses being offered, at the school, are necessary to help students learn the right stuff.
4. Decide what courses need to be added or redistributed in order to teach students information that they need to know to score well on state and national assessments.
5. Attach the information students need to know to score well on the standardized tests to specific courses to make sure that all information is to be covered in one course or another (Teachers should know which courses cover which specific descriptors).
6. Group the descriptors by course and by quarter so that the descriptors are grouped into the ones that will be covered in each quarter in each course.
7. Create quarterly assessments for each course that covers state descriptors.

The courses offered ought to be offered for the right reasons and not just because the teacher likes the topic. For instance, in some places it has been discovered that teachers spend weeks on "pet units" such as units about dinosaurs, the Civil War, or the Plains Indians. The fact of the matter is that there are usually not many questions on state or national tests about dinosaurs, the Civil War or The Plains Indians. Just because the teachers like to talk about such topics and students like studying such topics does not necessarily justify spending an exorbitant amount of time on the topics. Most of the time in classes might be better spent on teaching information that the student will need to know to score well on the state and national assessments. Collaborative teams might discover that the correct course that covers the right information is offered, but students are not scheduled to take the course until after they take the standardized tests. In such cases, the course needs to be redistributed on the schedule.

Some people like to complain about the state tests and tests in general. They say that teaching to the test is counter to good education practices. However, if we say that we want students to know a specific collection of concepts then I am a proponent of purposefully teaching in ways that helps students learn these concepts. Other information or concepts important for students to know may also be included, but the targeted concepts and information should have the priority. It is the responsibility of educators to create a process to prepare students so that they will have positive choices in post-secondary life.

# Chapter 12
# Design Assessment-Based Instruction

To design assessment-based instruction, collaborative cooperative teams need to create quarterly common assessments based on the state descriptors. Afterward individual teachers could create six smaller tests from information on the common assessment. The individual teachers could then design the lesson units around the six smaller tests. By making sure that they teach the students exactly what they want the students to know and testing the students on what they taught them, (making sure there are no tricks), teachers build trust between themselves and students. Teachers may teach students a wide variety of information and test them overall on some of the information taught, but be consistent at not testing students on information not taught or assigned.

After the collaborative teams have agreed on questions and answers on the common assessment, individual teachers would divide the information covered on the common assessment into six smaller tests unique to the style of individual teachers. The individual teachers would design lesson units around the six smaller tests. Teachers could create effective units by answering these questions:

- Which part of the quarterly common assessment does this unit cover?
- Which of the state frameworks does this unit match?
- What do I want the students to know as a result of this unit?
- If this unit was finished, what three to five concepts in every lesson would I want to be sure the students remembered?
- How does this unit address the school improvement plan?
- How will I determine student readiness for the unit test?
- What methods and materials will I use to teach the lessons in this unit?
- How will I know whether the students learned the three to five concepts or procedures I wanted them to learn?

# DEVELOPING THE ASSESSMENT-BASED INSTRUCTION DESIGN MODEL
## (A three- to five-year endeavor)

## Core Curriculum Teams Should:

1. Review the common assessments for each quarter in each core curriculum course.
2. Divide the information in each quarterly assessment into groups of six.
3. Cover each group of information in one week of lessons.
4. Divide each group of information to be taught in a week into four sections.
5. Design daily lessons around each section of information.
6. Design weekly tests that assess how much information students have internalized about the four sections of information taught per week.
7. Review the results of the weekly tests to determine the pieces of information students may not have mastered.
8. Determine what strategies will be used to recover the information for the students and how the recovery will be assessed.

## Core Curriculum Teams Develop Test Questions On Each Week's Assessment:

| Unit Test 1 | Unit Test 2 | Unit Test 3 | Unit Test 4 | Unit test 5 | Unit Test 6 |
|---|---|---|---|---|---|
| Cover | Cover | Cover | Cover | Cover | Cover |
| Questions 1-20 | Questions 21-41 | Questions 42-62 | Questions 63-83 | Questions 84-104 | Questions 105-120 |
| 1st week | 2nd week | 3rd week | 4th week | 5th week | 6th week |

## Unit Test Design (See Above Diagram)

1. Each unit test should cover the information represented by each 20 questions on the quarterly common assessments.
2. Each unit should last four days and on the fifth day a unit test should be given.
3. Each group of 20 questions should be divided into sections of four so that teachers could design daily lessons around the sections.
4. Most quarters last eight weeks; two weeks should be set aside for possible administrative interruptions such as snow days, disaster drills, assemblies, and recovery and enrichment days.
5. By the end of each quarter all of the groups of information and the sections of information should have been covered.
6. By the end of each quarter recovery for struggling students and enrichment for achieving students should have been initiated.
7. By the end of each quarter students should be ready to score well on the quarterly assessments.
8. Quarterly assessments should be used to determine which students are struggling; then recovery strategies should be initiated for those students.

9. The quarterly assessments should be designed so that they give an indication as to how the students might fair on the state tests.

Data that comes directly from teacher-given assessments could be used by educators to help assess student learning and help teachers gauge the student's progress concerning how he or she might achieve on the common assessment. A student's performance on quarterly common assessments can give teachers advanced notice concerning how prepared or under-prepared students are for the state test. By taking into account the percentage of students passing the common assessments, teachers can evaluate their own effectiveness. When educators plan effective pedagogy, students will have higher achievement; input does influence output.

# DELIVERY OF INFORMATION STRATEGIES

Individual teachers should prepare lessons in their own individual styles that teach to the different learning styles of individual students. Teachers that teach to a variety of learning styles create opportunities to reach all students in his or her classes. More of the students within a class focus on the lesson when lessons are delivered in a variety of learning styles.

The four components of the learning style quadrants offer teachers a great way to remember to reach all four learning styles within lessons. Hanson, Silver, Young, and Strong modified this from the Myers Briggs learning styles information; this chart synthesizes the Hanson, Silver, Young and Strong model, the brain research by Dr. Bernice McCarthy, collaborative learning strategies of David and Roger Johnson, and cultural learning preferences by Dr. Janice Hale Benson.

## Cooperative Learning and Styles
### Modified from Hanson, Silver, Young and Strong
### Cooperative Learning Rules David and Roger Johnson 1999

| Left Brain<br>Dr. Bernice McCarthy | | Right Brain<br>Dr. Bernice McCarthy |
|---|---|---|
| **Practical**<br><br>**Individual Accountability**<br><br>• Each one contributes to reaching the goal | Vocational & Technical Prep | **Interactive**<br><br>**Face-to-Face Interaction**<br><br>• Helping each other learn; applauding success and effort |
| **Logical**<br><br>**Group Accountability**<br><br>• The team is collectively responsible for goal achievement | College Prep | **Creative**<br><br>**Positive Interdependence**<br><br>• Sink or swim together in win-win relationships |
| Analytical<br>Dr. Janice Hale Benson | | Relational<br>Dr. Janice Hale Benson |

121

## Hanson, Silver, Young, and Strong:

The partners in this educational consulting firm condensed the multiple learning style indicators of Myers Briggs into four quadrants. They determined that four quadrants offer teachers more ease throughout day-to-day teaching than 16 or more learning style indicators of the Myers Briggs. The four quadrants of practical, logical, interactive and creative have been modified for the purposes of this book but they reflect the spirit of Hanson, Silver, Young, and Strong:

* Practical learners like sensible, realistic, no-nonsense, and matter-of-fact lessons.
* Logical learners like rational, reasonable, sound, commonsensical, consistent, coherent, and valid lessons.
* Interactive learners like lessons to involve participation, association, connection with others, teaming, and partnering.
* Creative learners like imaginative, inspired, inventive, artistic, ingenious, resourceful, innovative, and productive lessons.

When students learn to believe that they can accomplish tasks no matter how unachievable the task may at first seem, nothing can hold them back. After learning the art of "little chunks," students become proficient at breaking down big projects so they can complete one little chunk at a time, and before they know it the whole job is finished and it doesn't seem so difficult after all.

## Dr. Bernice McCarthy:

Dr. McCarthy suggested that teachers begin to understand how the brain learns and that some students may rely on one side of the brain more than they do the other in terms of learning. She suggested students preferring lessons appealing to left brain learning prefer practical and logical lessons, while students that prefer lessons that appeal to right brain learning prefer interactive and creative lessons. Dr. McCarthy also cautioned that the ideal student would be a whole brain learner— one exposed to lessons that introduce all four quadrants.

## David and Roger Johnson:

The Johnson brothers advocate cooperative learning strategies and suggest that several rules must be employed that differentiates cooperative learning from group work. The chart above shows how a modification of these rules would fit into the learning styles quadrants. Each of the four rules would mesh with at least one of the learning styles quadrants, thus creating intellectual compatibility with students who embrace the same learning style quadrant.

## Dr. Janice Hale Benson:

Dr. Hale-Benson suggested that gender and culture play a role in learning. In her books, Dr. Hale-Benson explained that most boys usually prefer lessons that appeal to left brain learning. When teachers employ practical and logical techniques, they will reach most of the boys in class. Most girls however usually prefer lessons that appeal to right brain learning. When teachers employ interactive and creative techniques, they will reach most of the girls in class. Dr. Hale-Benson goes further in explaining that most American-white students and most American-Asian students prefer lessons that appeal to the left brain learner, while most American-black students and most other minority students prefer lessons that appeal to the right brain learner.

## Vocational and Technical Prep Students:

Most students preparing for technical post-high school programs usually prefer practical and interactive lessons. They like sensible, realistic, no-nonsense, matter-of-fact lessons, which at the same time involve participation, association, connection with others, teaming, and partnering.

## College and Advanced Technical Prep Students:

Most students preparing for college and university post-high school programs usually prefer logical and creative lessons. They like rational, reasonable, sound, commonsensical, consistent, coherent, and valid lessons; but at the same time they like imaginative, inspired, inventive, artistic, ingenious, resourceful, innovative, and productive lessons.

Of course, not all students fit easily into categories as suggested, but enough of them have the characteristics for these generalizations to make it worthwhile to discuss. If teachers begin to keep these ideas in mind as they construct lesson plans, it will make school a more enjoyable place for everyone involved and students will probably learn and understand more, faster.

## THE TAXONOMY OF QUO

EnTeam Executive Director Ted Wohlfarth introduced a reorganization of the Bloom taxonomy that dovetails nicely with the four quadrants learning styles chart. He emphasizes debriefing for Critical Thinking Skills and suggests that in order to develop critical thinking skills, teachers should start with events that challenge students to draw on their creativity and curiosity. Teachers might then debrief the experiences to encourage students to generalize the specific activity into broader principles and applications.

| Knowledge of the facts<br><br>*Who? What?<br>Where? When?<br>How? Why?* | **Comprehension**<br>Understand the facts in the context of the particular situation.<br><br>*Compare, contrast, explain, extend, summarize* | **Analysis**<br>Take apart<br>Probe the causes and motives behind the facts in the particular situation and how they might be generalized to other contexts and related to universal principles. | **Evaluation**<br>Draw conclusions and make choices using the principles identified in analysis and synthesis.<br><br>*Appraise, award, decide, choose, interpret, prioritize, value, devalue, conclude* |
|---|---|---|---|
| | **Application**<br>Use the comprehension of the facts in a similar situation.<br>*Apply, build, experiment, interview, organize* | **Synthesis**<br>Put together again<br>Make connections between the facts and principles in relationship to a broader context. Look extensions of the particular to the general. Discover patterns and new applications or solutions. | |
| | **Specific context** | **General context and perspective** | |

Adapted from Benjamin Bloom, *Taxonomy of Educational Objectives: The Classification of Educational Goals: Handbook I, Cognitive Domain,* 1956

## Open-ended questions to lead students through The Taxonomy:

- What happened? [knowledge]
  - -- *What are the facts in this experience?*
  - -- *What makes this experience important?*
  - -- *What lessons did you learn from this experience?*

- So what? [Practical, logical, interactive, and creative]
  - -- *What are some of the principles at work in this experience?*
  - -- *How may the facts in this experience be compared and contrasted?*
  - -- *How do the principles in this experience apply in other situations?*

- Now what? [evaluation]
  - -- *How could we improve our performance if we had this experience again?*
  - -- *Given this experience, what implications do you see for your choices or decisions?*
  - -- *What actions or opportunities are worth considering?*
  - -- *If a sequence can be established what might happen next and into the future?*

Sometimes changing to an efficient and effective way of doing things proves difficult. For instance, when a tennis player teaches himself or herself how to serve, the technique that he or she uses may be usable and even comfortable, but not effective or efficient. When this same person acquires a coach, the proper way to serve may seem awkward at first. The player may even revert to the makeshift serve from time to time when he or she gets frustrated, but if the player wants his or her serve to be consistently effective, then he or she must conform to the rules for effective serving.

In applying the tennis serve analogy to education, many teachers that first begin to use Learning Styles-Centered Instruction, fortified by the taxonomy of QUO, resist the change. At first, this method may seem time-consuming or confining, but as the teacher begins to use this process, the learning curve of students increases dramatically. An increase in learning among students also positively impacts student behavior. When students are required to learn, they have less time or desire to get involved with negative behaviors.

# Learning Styles Delivery
## Modified from Hanson, Young, and Strong

| **Left Brain**<br>*Dr. Bernice McCarthy* | **Right Brain**<br>*Dr. Bernice McCarthy* |
|---|---|
| **Practical**<br>(Guided Practice, Solve Problems Mastry Learning, Take Notes, Recite Introduction, Recovery Activities) | **Interactive**<br>(Individual Interest, Intellectual Regard, Cooperative Learning Proximity, Responsiveness, Use Names, Respect Diversity, Rapport, Equitable Distribution) |
| **Logical**<br>(Sequencing, Linking, Debate, Interpret, Research, Tutoring, Give Speech, Projects, Research Paper, Laboratory, Writing, Concept Mapping) | **Creative**<br>(Enrichment Activities, Guest Speaker, Brainstorming, Jigsaw, Conceptual Learning, Music, Create Portfolio, Carousel, Visual Enhancers, Closure) |
| **Analytical**<br>*Dr. Janice Hale-Benson* | **Relational**<br>*Dr. Janice Hale-Benson* |

# SYSTEMATIC LESSON DELIVERY MODEL

## Offer a Lesson Introduction For 10 Percent or Less of the Time Available For the Lesson:

Each lesson that a teacher delivers ought to have an introduction that takes 10 percent or less of the time available for the class period. Sometimes teachers become so anxious to get into their lessons that they zoom past the introduction and students miss out on the breakfast of the "lesson meal." Some nutritionists have said that breakfast is the most important meal of the day because it energizes the body's metabolism. Like breakfast for the body, the introduction jump starts the brain and gets it ready to receive the lesson. In this part of the lesson teachers explain the objectives and goals to the students and get them interested by using a variety of methods to help them get acclimated. This portion of the lesson helps students see the direction the period will take.

## State Objectives, Goals, Introduction, and Expectations:

- Discover prior knowledge
- Use kindling exercises
- Introduce opening vignettes
- List objectives or goals (four or less per lesson)

## Use Teacher Strategies for 30 Percent or Less of the Time Available for the Lesson:

Teachers provide expert information about the subject, but this portion of the lesson should take 30 percent or less of the allocated time for the class. This is the lunch portion of the "lesson meal." People that work and students take lunch in the middle of the day; following lunch they get right back to work. Teachers need to remember to make sure that there is time for students to practice right after teacher input. Teachers sometimes get so involved in delivering subject matter that they lose track of time. Teachers must avoid spending too much time delivering information so students can get a chance to practice what they are learning. Teachers can use a variety of strategies to deliver information to students.

## Within the Presentation Component Teachers Can Use:

- Latency (wait-time), affirmation, personal warmth
- Equitable distribution, metaphorical sharing
- Questions, comprehension check
- Overheads, PowerPoint
- Lecture
- Graded materials

Teachers may lecture, ask questions, and share metaphoric explanations to help students understand. To engage students, teachers can use equitable distribution, discussion, affirmation, latency, and show personal warmth toward the students to help them embrace lessons.

## Use Student Production Methods 50 Percent or More of the Time Available For the Lesson:

Students could practice for at least 50 percent or more of the time allotted for the lesson. In the dinner of the "lesson meal," students work more leisurely and do have to finish at a particular time. Teachers can use this part of the lesson to give students practice and explain the lesson in more depth.

## During the Student Production Component Teachers Could Use:

- Cooperative groups, pairs, jigsaw, Yahma, fishbowl, round-robin carousel
- Brainstorming, discussion

- Lab assignments, debate
- Handouts to be completed or studied
- Games
- Music

Practice during lessons could help students unify as a class. Teachers could create incentives for students; everyone in class could be rewarded when the class is successful at working together to achieve goals.

## Use Closure Methods 10 Percent or Less of the Time Available for the Lesson:

Teachers should draw closure to the lesson during the final 10 percent or less of the time allotted for lessons. In the dessert of the "lesson meal," students can determine connections within the lesson and discover how the lesson relates to lessons in the past and can anticipate how the lesson will relate to lessons in the future.

## During the Cosure Component Teachers Can Use:

- Preview
- Review
- Summarize
- Link
- Quizzes

# Chapter 13
# Motivation from Cooperative Learning

*"Teaching and learning must be personalized so that teachers are able to help with construction of knowledge."*

Thomas J. Sergiovanni, *Leadership for the Schoolhouse*

### "Could You Talk to Her?"
The students had come to the office during passing period to have a talk with me. My secretary asked them to have a seat because I was in a meeting with a parent and a staff member. When the meeting was finished my secretary beckoned for the three girls to enter my office. The girls were neatly dressed, well groomed, and all three were under 5'3" tall; maybe 5'0" or 5'1."

The spokesperson for the group was LaWanda Simpson, the one with the darkest coloration. She was very matter of fact as she spoke, *"Dr. Harris we've got to talk to you about Mrs. Watson, she needs help."* I asked the girls to come in and have a seat.

I said, *"I know you LaWanda, but I don't believe I've met your friends."*

LaWanda introduced them, *"This is Carmeletta Jones and Corliss Degraphenreid."*

I shook hands with both girls and said, *"Nice to meet you. Now what can I do for you young ladies? "*

Corliss had a fair complexion, dark brown eyes, and shoulder length brown hair. Carmeletta had medium brown skin, light brown eyes, and long braid extensions in her hair. LaWanda had decorative braids with a specific design tight to her head. All three girls were small in size and weight. I remembered seeing Corliss and Carmeletta on the freshman girl's basketball team and LaWanda was in the choir and on the Student Advisory Board.

Carmeletta said, *"It's Algebra Dr. Harris. We don't get it. It don't make no sense."*

Corliss said, *"Yeah, I don't see what good it is anyway but I need to know this stuff if I'm going to move on to Algebra II after Geometry. I have got to go to college, don't cha know."*

I asked, *"Why do you think you are having a problem? What are the other students that understand doing in the class?"*

LaWanda said, *"Ain't nobody getting it cause that lady cannot teach. Now I have a 3.5 grade point average and Carmeletta and Corliss both have better grades than me. So I usually do pretty well, but this lady is a horrible teacher."*

I could see that the girls were determined. I asked, *"What is happening in the class that makes you think the teacher has a problem? Maybe the students are not doing homework or are not paying attention."*

*"Now Dr. Harris, how can everybody be not paying attention?"* LaWanda frowned as she continued, *"And LaWanda does her homework every night. I'm telling you this woman cannot teach. I do not get why she moves from one thing to the other and I have no clue as to when something ends and a new thing begins."*

Corliss said, *"If you don't believe us you should go see for yourself. Just please don't tell her that it was us who said something about her. She gets real mad real easy, don't cha know."*

*"She makes you feel stupid when you ask a question and she calls us names like ignorant and dumb."* Carmelletta looked down at her hands as the sentence trailed to its end.

LaWanda said, *"I wasn't going to bring that up but you know LaWanda don't put up with that kind of disrespect. If she ever calls me anything like that my mamma will be up here in a hot minute."*

Corliss said, *"Could you talk to her? Go watch her teach and you will see what we mean, Dr. Harris. The lady just can't teach."*

The students probably did not know it but they were not the first students who had come to complain about Mrs. Watson. Mrs. Watson was a 20-year veteran teacher who had probably mentally retired about five years earlier. I had visited her class earlier in the year and had talked with her about changing her style and implementing some of the strategies that had been discussed in the staff development sessions.

Each time we talked Mrs. Watson assured me that she would try different techniques but I feared that she never would. By talking to the girls it seemed that I was correct. I wrote on my calendar to visit Mrs. Watson's class the next day.

When I visited Mrs. Watson's class, she spent the entire period lecturing. She was so excited about algebra that the departure bell caught her in mid-sentence; there was no closure, nor had there been objectives at the beginning for that matter. I'm sure that another mathematician would have been fascinated by her soliloquy, but I'm sure the students were less than fascinated; many of them were working hard to stay awake. Some teachers find it difficult to avoid continuously using the lecture method. The lecture method is not always well received by students and many students find a constant diet of this method boring. The cooperative learning method of delivery has many of the strategies and techniques already mentioned embedded within its construct.

# ORGANIZING COOPERATIVE LEARNING

The use of cooperative learning teams could be so comprehensive that many of the other methods are inherent in the process. To address the academic motivational needs of students that prefer left brain endeavors individual accountability and face-to-face interaction could be required. To address the academic motivational needs of students that prefer right brain endeavors, group accountability and positive interdependence could be required. Those students that have a propensity toward analysis will probably gain motivation within the cooperative learning construct because of the individual accountability and face-to-face interaction requirement; while students that enjoy interactive lessons could gain motivation within the cooperative learning construct because of the group accountability and positive interdependence requirement.

Teachers may find that by using cooperative teams the academic motivational needs of students that look for the practical element could be satisfied because the team would be partially guided by rules that require individual accountability. The academic motivational needs of students that look for the logical element could be satisfied because the team would be partially guided by rules that require face-to-face interaction. Those students that are motivated by interaction would be satisfied because the team would be partially guided by rules that require group accountability. The academic motivational needs of students that look for the creative element could be satisfied because the team would be partially guided by rules that require positive interdependence.

To organize the practice of cooperative learning, rules could be required that address the practical, logical, interactive, and creative learning styles of all of the students. The success of the team would depend on each of the students contributing to the attainment of the team goals. Further, team success would depend on members helping each other and applauding the success and effort of teammates. A degree of individual success would depend on the team's achievement; teammates would understand that they would either sink are swim together. No success would be total for an individual if the team does not succeed and no team gains complete success if one of the individuals on the team is not successful.

First, the team members would select a spokesperson that would be the "voice" of the group. The spokesperson would push for clarity of information, preciseness, and lucidity. Information to be shared with the entire group would be spoken only by the spokesperson. The group would also select a troubleshooter to be the "taskmaster" of the group. The troubleshooter would monitor the activities of the group making certain that everyone stay on task and complete the task in a timely matter as completely and with as much quality as possible within the time constraints.

## Basic Cooperative Learning Techniques:

1. Jigsaw Techniques
   - Meet in basic groups—each group becomes expert on one concept.
   - New groups are formed that contain one expert from each basic group.
   - Each group member teaches other group members the information in which he or she has formed an expertise.

2. Carousal Technique
   - Basic groups work together to place concepts or information on poster paper.
   - Basic groups attach poster paper to different locations on the walls in the room.
   - Basic groups then move from one posting to the other, on command, spending time at each poster discussing the information on the poster paper.
   - Basic groups then meet again to synthesize the information and make connections.
   - Basic groups then share out thoughts.

3. Fishbowl Technique
   - Two circles (one smaller inner circle and a larger outer circle) would be formed which include everyone in class.
   - The inner circle discusses topics that have been introduced by the instructor.
   - The outer circle listens and takes notes so that they can formulate ideas concerning what was discussed.
   - The outer circle discusses their perceptions of what was communicated while those in the inner circle listen and take notes.

4. Round Robin Technique
   - Groups of students take turns working in pairs within the groups.
   - The effectiveness of the teamwork is scored.

5. Yahma Technique
   - Everyone in the class is placed in a large circle.
   - Each person is offered an opportunity to express their opinions on a topic of focus.
   - Individuals may decline or postpone responding.

# Part Six
# To Assure Quality, Manage Direct Data

- *Identify struggling students and high achievers*

- *Create recovery techniques for struggling students and enrichments for high-achieving students*

# Chapter 14
# Managing Direct Data

*"The best indicator of what a student knows is the work itself. The work of students is important and should comprise a record to be revisited by teachers and students, a record to be used for further teaching and assessment, and a record to be shared with parents."*

Thomas J. Sergiovanni, *Leadership for the Schoolhouse*

## Manage Direct Data for the Custodial Components

Teachers and administrators should collect data on both the custodial component and the academic component of school organization. Teachers and administrators should identify students that are struggling behaviorally and academically. Students that choose to be challengers will have a difficult time negotiating school, learning, and getting good grades; therefore challengers need to be confronted immediately, consistently, and relentlessly. They must be required to take responsibility for their refusal to abide by the rules and guidelines of the school. Students must understand that inappropriate behavior will be followed by swift consequences.

> **Students must understand that inappropriate behavior will be followed by swift consequences**

Administrators and teachers should collect data on students that undergo consequences to determine if the consequences are changing behaviors; use the MCER method. For instance, measure by determining, how many students are assigned after school detention, assigned to in-school detention, are assigned 10 day suspensions, or have received an expulsion. Compare the results to the results from previous years, previous semesters, and quarters of school. Administrators and teachers must then be willing to make revisions to the discipline system after reviewing the data. Make an evaluation by answering these questions:

- Is general behavior improving?
- Is behavior improving by grade level?
- Is behavior improving more among girls or boys?
- How are consequences affecting individual students?

Use the information from the data to determine if students that enter the discipline system have improved grades on the successive grade reports. Determine if the students that do not frequent the discipline system have improved grades as the number of discipline consequences of the challengers increase. This information would give some indication as to whether receiving consequences helps improve the overall academic production of the challengers and if removing the challengers from class helps improve the academic progress of the other students. The results of such information can be used to revise the consequence system, revise parts of the discipline system, or revise the entire discipline system.

## Example Letter to Parents About Discipline Situation:

*November 22, 2004*

*Dear Parents,*

*It is distressing to report that Darla White has been placed in In-School-Suspension 10 times or more for violations of the discipline code or other inappropriate behavior at school. Darla White has also earned 5 Fs on the last grade report. At Cahokia High School students are expected to behave appropriately, display good manners and civility and achieve Cs or better in all classes. When a student receives failing grades and is constantly involved in the discipline system it is a signal to parents and educators that the student is refusing services and is not matriculating toward high school graduation.*

*Because your youngster is consistently involved in the discipline system, continuous discipline interventions have become cumbersome and do not seem to be modifying the behavior of your child. **The behavioral interactions for your child from this point forward will be escalated to suspension status. When your child chooses to display behaviors that lead to placement in ISS, out-of-school suspension will occur instead. Suspensions will begin with two days and escalate by one upon each successive referral to ISS.***

*I am concerned that your youngster is refusing to conform to the expectations at Cahokia High School. I am asking that you help get the point across to your youngster as to the behavioral and academic expectations at Cahokia High School. Perhaps you, Darla, and I need to discuss strategies that will more effectively lead toward success. If you agree and would like to meet, please set an appointment by phoning my secretary Mrs. Althea Ross (618-333-3333 ext. 3333).*

*I hope that this information helps you in your efforts to monitor your child's educational progress.*

*Sincerely,*
*Dr. Ed Harris*
*Principal Cahokia High School*

## Manage Direct Data for the Academic Components

To gain quality of student learning in schools, educators can use data to identify both students that are struggling academically and students that are high academic achievers. On the low end, what may be just as important is to distinguish the students that are struggling because they simply do not comprehend from the students that refuse to apply effective effort.

The important question on the high end is to distinguish students that score high because they are "exceptional" from students that score high because they are proficient at doing teacher-pleasing behaviors and are relentless about consistency of study, dedication to quality work, and regularity of assignment completion.

These differentiated groups need different types of interventions. On the low end, students that have difficulty comprehending need a different kind of intervention than do students that refuse services. Students that do not try might need alternative forms of motivation and some might need to be in a different setting from the other students.

On the high end, the exceptional students might need additional challenge more than they need activities that bring praise and recognition, while the unrelenting quality-seeking students might need activities that bring praise and recognition more than they need additional challenge. Making these determinations is intricate; educators that begin to make these determinations need to closely investigate the available data that already exists in the district and in individual buildings within districts. However, the most prolific information is probably in the memory of teachers that have worked with the students previously. Different teacher teams, set-up within the district, triangular looping dyads, core curriculum teams, and operational collectives could make determinations concerning the identification of the four levels of academic achievement on the high and low end of the spectrum.

Interventions could be implemented for all four groups. Educators could have predetermined interventions they will use as recovery strategies to help struggling students and enrichment techniques for the high achieving students. Teams of elementary school teachers and teams of secondary teachers could introduce interventions in individual classrooms and operational collectives could introduce programs for interventions that could serve as a comprehensive guidepost for the entire district.

## Letter to Parents About an Academic Situation

*April, 2005*

*Dear Mrs. Adobe,*

*Your son, Charles Adobe, has been placed on the Academic Watch List due to lack of academic effort. Being placed on the Academic Watch List indicates that a student has passed only three classes or less on a six-class schedule. The situation would reveal that the student has received three or more failing grades on the most recent grade report.*

*Students placed on the Academic Watch List are in effect "grounded" by the administration. Placement on the Academic Watch List disallows the student's participation in or attendance at all extracurricular activities. Students that are placed on the Academic Watch List will also be excluded from all-school assemblies, Prom, and other privileges extended to students in good standing.*

*The teachers of students that have been placed on the Academic Watch List have been contacted and instructed to closely monitor the student's academic performance:*

> *1. If a student on the Academic Watch List has difficulty understanding concepts the teacher should assign him or her to Academic Lab to acquire help.*

2. *If a student on the Academic Watch List does not turn in an assignment the student should be assigned by the teacher to after school detention until the assignment is completed and turned in to the appropriate teacher.*

*As the parent, guardian, or provider for this student, you, and the student could discuss the student's academic future and conceive a plan designed to help the student improve his or her academic performance and raise his or her grades.*

*Sincerely,*
*Dr. Ed Harris*
*Principal Cahokia High School*

# Chapter 15
# Identifying Struggling Students and High Achievers

## Elementary School Dyad Teams and Secondary School Teams Could Determine the Identification of:

- Students that refuse services
- Students with low comprehension
- Unrelenting quality-seeking students
- "Exceptional" students

Teachers within individual classrooms could collect data from the assessments that they use to check for the comprehension levels of their students. The teachers could design their assessment instruments with data collection in mind. The assessments could be designed so that collection of data will be less cumbersome for the teacher. One example would be to itemize, number, and categorize the assessment by concept so that if students answer two of five questions in a series, it would reflect that the student is experiencing difficulty with a specific concept. Tests could also be disaggregated (data that is separated in order to study the performance of various groups within a total population) by gender and race so that the teacher can determine if there are significant differences between learners in his or her class based on a student's externals. The main purpose of collecting academic data is to find ways to increase student learning by identifying students that do not understand the information and finding ways to help them learn.

It has been a common practice in many classrooms for teachers to teach information at a specific rate of speed and whether a student learned the information or not after

> The main purpose of collecting academic data is to find ways to increase student learning by identifying students that do not understand the information and finding ways to help them learn.

the unit test, the teacher would move on. However, when the curriculum has been authenticated and teaching teams are certain that the "right stuff" is being taught to the students, it is important that every effort is made to help all of the students gain at least a minimal level of understanding about the subject. Therefore, teacher-made assessments could be used as an indicator of how much students understand the information on the one hand and to identify students that are not learning on the other hand.

Consequently, to facilitate the teachers, recovery initiatives could be introduced at the school level. Teaching teams and individual teachers could also develop or adopt several strategies that could be used to help students learn. Teachers need to keep a few readily available techniques in their "Teaching Tool Boxes" that can be introduced immediately to help struggling students learn. Some strategies within their tool boxes could be universal tools—ones that any teacher on the learning team could use; but some could be designed by individual teachers to match individual teacher styles.

## Identifying Low Comprehension and Quality-Seeking Students

Testing and other forms of assessment could help teacher teams identify students that have low comprehension (LC) and quality-seeking (QS) students. LC students and QS students could probably have a positive impact on each other. After analyzing the results of assessments they have administered, individual teachers could create enrichments for students that understand the material and recovery for students that are struggling. Enrichment for QS students might be to tutor the struggling students. In this way both goals can be met for participating students.

Some QS students would probably find enjoyment in helping LC students learn and have a better understanding of information presented by the teachers. QS students usually are no strangers to hard work and like to see positive results from their work, especially if they receive recognition for their efforts. Consequently, QS students would probably make terrific tutors for LC students. LC students would probably be receptive to the help because they want to be able to understand the information presented. LC students and QS students often have the value of hard work in common and this commonality might help them form a bond when they study together.

Identifying LC and QS students is relatively less difficult as compared to identifying students who refuse services or are exceptional. Performance event assignments can be used, but not completely relied upon to determine the students that regularly refuse services or students that are exceptional; teacher intuition is needed as well.

## Identifying Exceptional Students and Students that Refuse Services

Exceptional students do not always make the top grades; sometimes there are large grade production swings, from very high to medium or sometimes low production. Low and medium grade production from exceptional students might be caused by a lack of challenge or imagination in the material or assignment which will cause boredom. Students that refuse services are not necessarily slow, dumb, or intellectually challenged; students that refuse services might even be exceptional. The problem is that they are students that refuse to give effective effort, therefore they struggle academically.

Exceptional students and students that refuse services are more of a challenge to teachers than are LC and QS students. Teacher teams could collaborate to create strategies and techniques that might serve as a hook to gain the attention and buy-in from the exceptional students. Once exceptional students embrace a subject or the charisma of a teacher, the door is opened for an explosion of his or her intellectual achievement. When the exceptional student is identified and the teacher team purposefully designs activities especially for them, the exceptional students will respond and reach to higher intellectual levels.

Teacher responses to students that refuse services are probably the most difficult. It is extremely perplexing for educators when students arrive at school with no intentions to learn the academic information; it is hard for teachers to teach a person against the person's will.

Students that refuse services are a detriment not only to him or her, but are also trouble for their classmates. Students that refuse services are in effect being insubordinate because they are refusing to do what the teachers are asking of them. Sometimes students that refuse services become a disadvantage to classroom climate; it is not uncommon to find that some students that refuse services are negative influences on the other students. Teacher teams might decide that students that refuse services would best serve themselves by moving to a different placement; teachers could counsel them toward either an alternative school or pursuit of a GED.

# Chapter 16
# Creating Recovery Techniques for Struggling Students and Enrichments for High-Achieving Students

*"In the Chinese language, two characters represent the word 'learning.' The character means 'to study.' It is composed of two parts: a symbol that means 'to accumulate knowledge' is placed above a symbol for a child in a doorway. The second character means 'to practice constantly,' and it shows a bird developing the ability to leave the nest. The upper symbol represents flying; the lower symbol youth. For the Asian mind, learning is ongoing. 'Study' and 'practice constantly,' together, suggest that learning should mean: 'mastery of the way of self-improvement.'"*

Peter Senge, *A Fifth Discipline Resource: Schools That Learn*

### "I'm in This for the Students."
*Some of the teachers on staff did not like Mrs. Quickstep. The general feeling among her detractors was that she was trying to make the rest of the staff "look bad" or that she was "playing up to" the principal. The students and parents loved Mrs. Quickstep because she was all about what was best for student learning. Every week she selected 10 students from her five classes and she would call their homes to give their parents updates on the academic progress of the selected students.*

*Mrs. Quickstep would tell everyone who would listen that she was more interested in having the students understand what she was teaching than she was in how far along she moved in the text. She invested much of her time checking for comprehension. Mrs. Quickstep created a variety of ways to assess student understanding.*

143

*Mrs. Quickstep and her two colleagues that shared teaching biology created four common assessments, one for each quarter, and agreed to purposefully prepare their students to reach a certain benchmark when they take the tests. Mrs. Quickstep prepared lessons—some that lasted a week, and some that lasted two weeks. The lessons were packed with important information. There were continuous comprehension checks that were both graded and not graded.*

*Mrs. Quickstep explained to me that the frequent comprehension checks were her personal mental data on each one of her students. She explained that the data from the comprehension checks gave her the information that she needed to discover which students did not understand the information and which students did understand the information. She told me that she would spend extra time with the students who did not understand so that they would not be left behind. She said it gave her a chance to also do some creative, lesson-enhancing activities with the other students that did understand the information.*

*I liked the way that Mrs. Quickstep phoned the parents of students to keep the parents abreast of the progress of students and she made every student feel that what they learned in her class was important. Mrs. Quickstep said that she could accurately predict which students would score in which area on the common assessments and thus knew where students would probably score on the state assessment. No student "got over" (students who attempt to receive as much credit as possible for doing as little work as they can get away with) in Mrs. Quickstep's classes. Everyone was expected to learn and be smart and almost everyone met her expectations.*

*Of course every quarter more of Mrs. Quickstep's students would pass the common assessments than any of the students of the other teachers. She also had more students score at the highest levels. Students from Mrs. Quickstep's classes also scored very well on the state assessment. Because of her great teaching and tremendous relationship with students and parents Mrs. Quickstep won several awards from outside sources and her detractors were not happy about that.*

*Mrs. Quickstep is a fantastic teacher and she is doing nothing that cannot be duplicated by other teachers. If I had the power to make it happen, all of the teachers would be like Mrs. Quickstep. Mrs. Quickstep teaches smart and gets tremendous results. I felt sad that she was highly respected and even revered by people outside of the school but not held in the highest regard by all of her colleagues. When I expressed this to her she simply smiled, winked at me and said, "I'm in this for the students and I have a responsibility to their families to help them learn."*

Educators need to find ways to dispel the negativism that presents roadblocks that hamper the collaboration between those within the Learning Triad. When all three entities within the Learning Triad bond together, students learn at higher rates, parents and community members feel more empowered, and educators can engage more successfully in their craft. Input from all stakeholders helps those who make the decisions meet approval from a wider cross-section of constituents. Teams of teachers might best serve the students by concentrating on those students that want to learn.

Individual teachers might develop learning teams where students work together in collaborative groups to help all members understand concepts. Teachers

> **Teams of teachers might best serve the students by concentrating on those students that want to learn.**

could assign students to learning cohorts and encourage the cohorts to work together to make sure all members learn the information taught. Cohort members can have same class members or members from different class periods. Cohort members can be from classes of one teacher or be comprised of members from the classes of different teachers. Each teacher must utilize a strategy that works for him or her most effectively and that will most help student groups learn and understand concepts.

Operational collectives at the district level could facilitate teacher teams in the individual buildings by advocating the aggressive confrontation of students that refuse services. The district level operational collective could lay the course for building level operational collectives to set in place systems that would relentlessly deal with students that refuse services, by demonstrating poor attendance, ineffective effort, or insubordination. Building level operational collectives could ground (students restricted to participation only in academic activities) students that receive two or more failing grades on quarterly grade reports. Operational collectives could also design the discipline system so that it becomes a discipline issue when students do not attempt assignments that teachers have assigned.

Operational collectives could also design systems that facilitate teachers from all academic departments in their efforts to help struggling students get extra help. Teachers in the core curriculum and student tutors could be paid to stay after school and help students that have been assigned there for academic assistance. After-school study rooms help develop an atmosphere of academic focus by demonstrating to students and parents that the staff believes the core curriculum is important and relentlessly encourages students to give effective effort to learn and seek academic achievement. Students could be assigned to the study room by teachers or parents, or students could assign themselves to after-school study.

## SURVEYS PROVIDE A REALITY CHECK

There are several outside companies that produce computer software that address the emphasis that No Child Left Behind places on reading and math scores and ACT/SAT preparation. Another strategy that many high schools use is National Honor Society Peer Tutors. In many places students in National Honor Society must complete a number of hours of community service each year. When students in the National Honor Society are mobilized to tutor struggling students, they complete their obligation of community service at the same time they help classmates toward academic success.

A useful way to discover what parents and community members want of the schools and how they perceive schools is by developing a survey. The survey could be developed by an outside agency and distributed by mail with return addresses and postage already in place. If at least 50 percent of the stakeholders return the surveys, important information can be realized.

EnTeam, the organization created and directed by Ted Wohlfarth, is an outstanding source to shape and fashion a functional survey. EnTeam has provided such surveys for schools throughout the St. Louis, Missouri area and in many cases the results have been extremely insightful. Schools can use EnTeam surveys to provide additional information to help educators design better school atmosphere (see Figure 1 in the Appendix).

The sample survey in the Appendix is an example of a survey for parents; however, surveys could be given to students as well to discover how they are feeling about their learning opportunities at school. Much research has been done that support the idea that students learn more in atmospheres that they perceive are inviting and inclusive. It might be worthwhile for schools to survey the students to discover exactly what the feelings of the students are toward the school.

Also, individual teachers may be surprised at their findings if they were to give a pre-survey after the first two weeks of class and a post-survey during the last week of class. Teachers might learn enough from the surveys to implement improvements or revisions to their classes to help students feel more comfortable with learning opportunities. This effort to give students input might also give them a sense of power that would help them realize that they are important within the learning process and what they think matters. Parent and student surveys can help generate psychological adhesive to cement a strong, effective relationship between the people that comprise the Learning Triad.

Often parents and students feel overwhelmed by educators who are usually some of the most highly educated people in the community. Many of the parents and students feel intimidated by the official power of the school and believe that the educators will not listen to them and even feel that the educators do not care what

> **Parent and student surveys can help generate psychological adhesive to cement a strong, effective relationship between the people that comprise the Learning Triad.**

parents and students think concerning what should occur at the school.

To calm some of these attitudes the use of surveys would demonstrate that teachers could be courageous enough to extend invitations to parents and students to do informal evaluations of the delivery and style of the teacher. Teachers could collaborate with their teacher team partners to produce the instrument that all partners on the team would use for such evaluations. The evaluations could be distributed by individual teachers to their own students and the parents of their students. The evaluations could be anonymous and for the individual teacher's eyes only.

Other data that could be used to help improve instruction is when colleagues within teaching dyads and core curriculum teams evaluate each other to give helpful suggestions that will enhance the teaching of individual teachers and the teaching team as a whole. Along with the above-mentioned evaluations teachers should use self-evaluation techniques. This process of teacher evaluation would improve teaching, uplift student learning and help students score higher on teacher made tests, common assessments, and state and national assessments.

# EDUCATORS ARE THE LAST LINE OF DEFENSE

Individual teachers in individual classrooms have the opportunity to make a real difference. Educators must hold all American-black students accountable to the same standards as are other students. Educators must realize that in many cases the teacher acts as the only positive role model and mentor that some students see on a daily basis. Educators often hold the last line of defense against a lifetime of unsophisticated behavior, ignorance, and negativism that awaits uneducated students.

Educators can achieve quality within schools by insisting that students pursue academic excellence. The personal effort of each student plays a central role in closing the achievement gap. Students, especially American-black students, can realize that anyone can get smarter with hard work. Getting smarter brings deferred gratification that can last a lifetime. Each individual student could make certain that his or her effort matches or exceeds the expectations of the school and the teachers in individual classrooms. But most importantly, students, especially American-black students, can also demonstrate appropriate academic behavior, such as attentiveness in class, participation in subject-specific intellectual discourse, and commitment to studying on a regular schedule.

Several strategies aid school personnel when they implement plans to help students and teachers pursue academic excellence. An increase in advanced course offerings occurs when the strategies work. Grade-level grade point averages will increase. The administration will notice an increased demand for college and other post secondary education opportunities. The staff will notice that students achieve higher scores on state and national standardized tests.

## Institute Benchmark Grading and Have Students Sign on the Dotted Line

Individual educators and school districts as a whole would be innovative *not* to accommodate student failure by granting D or F grades. School districts could proudly proclaim that they do not accept anything less than effective effort from students. Educators know that anyone can get smart; all it takes is time and effort. School districts could embrace intellectualism and demand hard work from students. Teacher teams could create expectation statements for grading in each course and agree upon criteria for earning an A, B or C in the core curriculum.

Students contract for a specific grade at the beginning of the class. **Both the student and parent sign the contract.** The student holds to his or her contract and the teacher accepts nothing less than the contracted for work. If the student does not complete enough work or have the appropriate quality of work to attain at least a C, then the teacher records an incomplete on the student's record. The incomplete stays on the student's record until the student completes the work with significant quality to acquire a C, the grade contracted for, or better. Students can but do not have to retake classes; however, they have to do the work to get a grade and to get the credit. Educators should think of themselves as agents for students, preparing them to strive for the best they can reach and always place the positives of the students up front. As

147

a representation of the student, a transcript full of D's and F's send a horrible message about the student, the school, the school district, and the educators. Benchmark grading eliminates the proliferation of records filled with poor grades.

## The Positives of Benchmark Grading:

- Fewer students tardy to class
- A rise and then a deep drop in suspensions
- An initial number of requests for transfers out of the school followed by a larger number of transfers in

> **Educators should think of themselves as agents for students**

- A huge increase in effective effort by the general student population followed by a sharp increase in the GPAs of the students
- Parents and students begin to hold the scores on state and national standardized tests, credits earned, and GPAs as the main quantifiable measurement of learning and the main purpose of a school

## Enrichment and Recovery Day

After students take teacher-made tests and teachers grade the test and other materials, teachers could return and review everything with the students. Once teachers make the determinations concerning which students reached the benchmarks, the teachers could then take time for enrichment activities. For example, grant students that fall below the benchmark time for recovery and extra help. Students that receive A's or B's on the test could work on independent enrichment projects. Students that receive less than a C on the test could work on a recovery project to recover the knowledge at the teacher's direction or with an in-class tutor. Good tutors are usually C and B students.

## For Enrichments and Recovery Methods Use:

- Small peer- teaching groups
- Tutoring
- Role-play
- Outline
- Re-test

In the absence of motivation at home, educators have an opportunity to provide motivation and the implementation of a learning styles-based delivery model. This may help make lessons more interesting to a wider variety of students. When students are more interested in the subject matter at school and the lessons are more challenging, students will learn more, have more academic success, and there is less likelihood that students will drop out of school. Perhaps if dropping out of school could be curtailed, the billions spent on dropouts could be diverted to upgrading school facilities.

# Part Seven
# Reflections

# Chapter 17
# Letters to Stakeholders

*"Because education reform is a complex process that involves changing classroom practices, policymakers should avoid simple solutions to school improvement. How and why schools change their classroom practices may be more important than the selection of any particular reform type. Reform methods that allow educators to adapt their methods appear more successful than reforms with more fixed curriculum approaches. Thus, there is strong evidence from this study that it is important to encourage educators to focus on classroom practice when they choose and implement a reform model."*

Edward P. St. John, Genevieve Manset, Choog-Geun Chung, Glenda Droogsma Musoba, Siri Loescher, Ada B. Simmons, David Gordon, and Carol Anne Hossler, *"Comprehensive School Reform: an Exploratory Study," Reinterpreting Urban School Reform*, Louis Miron and Edward P. St. John, eds.

## "Good News Letter" I Was Happy to Send to the Parents:
*2005*

*Dear Parents of Cahokia High School students,*

*The students at Cahokia High School are on the move toward academic development. It is amazing the accomplishments the students have made in one year using QUO Process. For example, as you probably know, students that have three F's or more are placed on the Academic Watch list and grounded at school. In the first semester of 2004 there were **253** students on the Academic Watch List; this year that number decreased to **182** students on the Academic Watch List. In 2004 there were **108** upper classmen on the Academic Watch List; now only **66** upper classmen are on the Academic Watch List. In 2004 **41** freshmen students received all F's on their semester grade reports; this year only **15** freshmen received all F's on their semester grade reports.*

*As you can see from the data there is tremendous improvement on the low end, but there is also improvement on the high end. For instance, after the first semester of 2004 **137** students earned their way onto the honor roll; this year **196** students earned their way onto the honor roll. Also, seven students displayed that they are absolutely magnificent by earning straight A's on the first semester grade report for 2005. Furthermore, in order to be a true junior, students must earn 10 credits, two of which must be in English, and two of which must be in math. At the beginning of the year only **95** students met the criteria but after the first semester 58 additional students earned their way into the true junior category; now there are **153** true juniors at Cahokia High School.*

*Because of the improved work ethic, improved discipline during competition, and better attention and focus gained from higher academic achievement, there has been tremendous improvement in the sports program as well. Improvements include:*

* *Soccer – The best season in recent history*
* *Football – South 7 conference champs (first time in four years); 9-2 record (first time since 1993); made it to second round of state playoffs (first time in five years); three players made All-Metro.*
* *Girl's Basketball – Finished with a 12-11 record (second best record in school history); won two tournaments, one in Dupo and one at Gibault; one player is being strongly recruited by division I colleges.*
* *Boy's Basketball – (New Coach- Mr. Nash) beat Chicago Marist, ranked eighth in large schools; beat Althoff, ranked 4ᵗʰ in small schools; won fourth place in the Centralia Tournament; won second place in the Kansas Tournament; and we're Regional Champs.*
* *Wrestling (New Coach – Mr. Venne) had five state qualifiers and three alternates; finished with a 14-9 team record; were Conference Champs for the first time since 1995; are Regional Champs for first time since 1991; and we have a state champion for the first time in five years.*

*Students are beginning to understand that hard work and learning pays off. Parents, thank you for sending your students to school ready to learn with a message from you that gaining an education is of the highest priority and that educators are to be honored and respected. We appreciate your efforts. I ask that you call your child's favorite teacher today and thank him or her for their dedication to your child's academic and personal growth.*

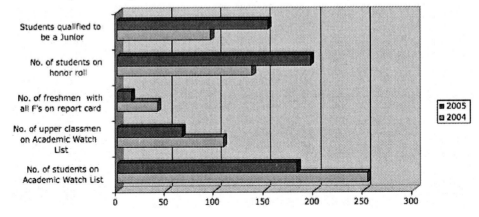

*Sincerely,*
*Dr. Edward Harris*
*Principal*

## Open Suggestion Letter to All Superintendents and Board Members in Low-Performing School Districts

*Dear Superintendents and School Board Members,*

*You may implement the QUO Process in a single school, but the most effective implementation is for the QUO Process to be articulated vertically, horizontally, and across the curriculum in the entire district. Everyone in the district could embrace the QUO Process so that it would follow a student from kindergarten to twelfth grade. Students should feel the cooperation of teachers from each core curriculum class to the enrichment classes as well. The QUO Process coordinates teachers so that student learning maximizes throughout the student's public education endeavor.*

*As a companion concept, educators could devise an aptitude test that eighth graders should take at the beginning of the second semester. The results of the test should be reviewed along with attendance, behavior, and earned academic records to determine in which direction educators recommend that individual students pursue. Conferences would be held with parents and students where educators would make their recommendations.*

*Students who demonstrate high aptitudes for college-bound studies would be recommended to move toward the four-year program. Students who demonstrate a high aptitude for vocational and technical studies would be recommended to pursue the three-year program. Students who demonstrate a struggle in traditional school settings would be recommended to pursue the GED.*

*Students eventually make these choices by chance anyway; it's just that schools have not designed programs that purposely address this issue.*

*Of course the parents should not be forced to accept the diagnosis of the educators, but at least they would have some idea of what direction the professionals felt would be right for individual students based on real data. After a year on the recommended path students could petition a committee to change to a different path if so desired. The committee would make a determination after a review of the record and reputation that the appealing student accumulated during the completed year. The parent and the student should be interviewed before a final decision is made.*

***Educators could make the process of getting an education more personal for students and parents when teacher teaming is combined with data-directed path determination.*** *In this way, educators could gain more ownership in a student's progress; students would have an opportunity to create stronger relationships with teachers; and parents would have access to the best thinking of the professionals that work with their unique children as to which direction would lead them to the most promising paths toward success. This system could strengthen relationships and feelings of belonging for the students and ownership of student achievement for teachers. Triangular and core curriculum team looping create the opportunity* *for closer relationships between parents and teachers. This enables lines of accountability and communication between teachers to be more tightly formed.*

*An unknown source has often been quoted when exploring management: "That which is monitored and evaluated is that which gets accomplished."*

*If we accept this line of thinking, then we must realize that a QUO Process specific evaluation instrument will help make the implementation of QUO Process more effective. Through their research, Ventures For Excellence Inc., a research firm, determined that excellent teachers definitely have similar characteristics:*

*1. **Excellent teachers have focus. They:***
- *Have and express specific personal purpose to help humanity through helping students grow and develop*
- *Purposely develop positive mentor-relationships with students*
- *Demonstrate concern and interest in learner outcomes*

*2. **Excellent teachers have four components in every lesson that:***
- *Communicate to the students in more than one way the objectives for the lessons*
- *Develop and use multiple teaching strategies during lesson delivery*
- *Help students discover ways to apply the lesson to their own personal living*
- *Specifically communicate, in the closure, the connections between the information delivery and the activities used.*

*3. **Excellent teachers aspire to motivate students by:***
- *Having high expectations in academics, character, and behavior*
- *supervising, monitoring, or coaching extra-curricular sports and activities or supporting students by attending extra-curricular sports and activities*
- *Being positive role models*
- *Giving themselves multiple options for delivery*
- *Having alternative methods of delivery*
- *Taking another route during the lesson when they discover that students do not understand.*

*4. **Excellent teachers show they care about students by:***
- *Focusing their attention on student growth and the importance of service to humanity*
- *Seeking to know as much as possible about their students including personal life, student life, and academic achievement*
- *Endeavoring to know student awareness and readiness levels before the lesson planning process begins*
- *Understanding the components or blueprints for developing strong lessons*
- *Attempting to have a positive impact on students by improving student behavior and cognition*

*When you hire certified staff members, insist that people with the above characteristics receive the highest priority. **Outstanding teachers hold the key to***

**good schools.** *As school leaders, you can do things both in the short run and in the long haul to make certain that everyone understands that you firmly resolve to take bold and innovative initiatives in your efforts to improve the quality of education and make a positive impact on student learning. Implementation of triangular and team looping could be a great help when encouraging focus, four component lessons, student motivation, and establishing an atmosphere of caring.*

*Obviously, some teachers think that the new interest and national regulations concerning high expectations and accountability in education amounts to mere talk and slogan chanting. Some veteran teachers believe that if student learning does not occur and if state test scores do not improve, then maybe the school board, the superintendent, and the other administrators will lose their jobs, but nothing will happen to teachers. Such teachers think that for them, business as usual will continue. They will collect their paychecks and move toward retirement literally unscathed. Their rallying cry: "This too shall pass."*

*However,* ***your best teachers understand and embrace the spirit of the current thinking about student achievement.*** *These teachers endeavor to find ways to help all students learn. Therefore, positive focus on teachers that present the characteristics of excellence and strive to motivate students to learn would prove most effective. Staff members would receive a clear understanding of expectations and administrators would be granted the mandate to put in place new creative ways to assess whether teachers met these expectations.*

### Explain the Plan

*You work against yourself when you hire teachers and then just release them to wander into the building with little or no direction, and without knowing the plan for the school. When they know the plan for the school, teachers within a building should be expected to develop and reveal their plan to protect the learning environment, apply systemic learning cycles, manage direct data, and create interventions for academic support within their classrooms. They should have at least two or more methods to facilitate each of the two strategies within each component. Teachers should also be expected to know how the administration will assist and support their efforts to address those components.*

*I recommend that the school districts where you serve embrace Collaborative School Transformation and that the Learning Triad within your districts embrace Quo Process. Those within your school districts that most religiously incorporate concepts of QUO Process should be rewarded.*

### Objective Rating System

*To compensate teachers who consistently use components of the QUO Process, initiate an objective rating system, such as the Results-Oriented Teacher Assessment instrument. With the completed evaluation, teachers would earn a rating average. Teacher pay could reflect the rating average so that the teachers who most consistently do what the QUO Process requires earn the most lucrative reward. For instance, the pay scale would not include a time-in-place category but instead would have a pay-by-*

*percentage component. To begin, everyone would start at current pay rates, but in the future, new hires would start at the entry level. The pay schedule might be as such:*

- *Teachers receiving a rating of 3.45 to 4. would receive 100 percent of the school board-approved pay increase.*
- *Teachers receiving a rating of 2.95 to 3.44 would receive 75 percent of the school board-approved pay increase.*
- *Teachers receiving a rating of 2.45 to 2.94 would receive 50 percent of the school board-approved pay increase.*
- *Teachers receiving a rating of .95 and 2.44 would receive 20 percent of the school board-approved pay increase. If a teacher in this category fails to move him or herself to proficiency (2.45 or above) within the year, then he or she would receive a "Failure to Reach Proficiency" notice. If he or she fails to reach proficiency one year after the notice, then the district would terminate him or her.*

*Teachers receiving a rating of 1.94 or below would receive no pay increase and would immediately receive a "Failure to Reach Proficiency" notice. If tenured, the district would grant one year to move performance to proficiency. If a teacher in this category failed to comply, then the district would terminate him or her. The district would terminate an untenured teacher in this category at the end of the school year.*

### Administrators could assess teachers using four lenses:
- *Teacher's personal point of view*
- *Student point of view*
- *Peer point of view*
- *Administrative point of view*

*Teachers would perform a self-assessment by using Standard 3 of the Results Oriented Teacher Accountability (ROTA) instrument. Teachers would offer students an opportunity to use Standard 4 of the ROTA (see Table 3 in the Appendix). Using Standard 1 of the ROTA, members of teacher teams would assess the accountability of its individual members. If the teacher does not belong to a teacher team, then he or she must petition for adoption by a teacher team to agree to act as peer evaluators. An administrator should assess teacher accountability by using Standard 2 of the ROTA.*

*The scores from all of the evaluations could be averaged for each person on each teacher team. Consequently, each teacher will receive a score in each of the four ROTA areas and a fifth score from the team. The five scores averaged for a teacher would produce a final score. The final score indicates the teacher's accountability rate and determines the teacher's pay increase and retention status. The department head or lead teacher would compile the evaluation information and present it to the administrator.*

*Teachers scoring in the top two categories would be evaluated every year. Teachers in the third scoring category would be evaluated every two years or upon the teacher's request at the beginning of the school year. Teachers in the third category could receive the same score over a two-year period if they do not request an evaluation that could possibly bring an upgraded score.*

*The implementation of the Results-Oriented Teacher Assessment instrument (see Table 2 in the appendix) would allow a broader system for evaluating the effectiveness of a teacher. The most effective teachers would receive more compensation therefore teachers might be motivated to strive for greater effectiveness. Objectivity would be the overwhelming attitude of the assessment as an effort to bring reward for quality to the teacher evaluation system.*

### Survey the Parents

*As a companion piece the administration could send surveys to parents for each teacher. Parents could have an opportunity to give input on the teachers as well. With information from representation of every group within the Learning Triad, a more concise and comprehensive evaluation could be established.*

### Accountable for Scores

*Research suggests that the most important component in making certain students learn is hiring and retaining good educators. More is required, however to raise test scores; when students are held accountable for their scores they will have more reason to do well on standardized tests.*

*Sincerely,*
*Dr. Edward Harris*
*Principal*

## Open Letter of Request to Government Officials

*Dear Government Leaders,*

*I admire the spirit of NCLB to motivate school districts and individual schools to academically uplift struggling students and to encourage states to give curriculum direction to schools. People within most school districts probably receive well the efforts toward motivation and encouragement. Furthermore, most educators probably welcome fair accountability measures.*

*However, tests do not reveal how much students learned in any of the disaggregated groupings tested. Many parents within school districts do not require or motivate their youngsters to do well on state tests. Parents and students generally understand the significance of national tests, especially parents that have college bound students. But the significance of the state tests appears nebulous at best to most parents and students.*

### Rebellion in the Ranks

*State tests have evolved into high-stakes assessment indicators of individual schools in each state.*

*"NCLB has made it so that state testing has actually become a whip placed in the hands of teenagers with which they can beat their teachers as they rebel against the system,"*

*says Katheryn Nelson, educator and former manager of school reform programs sponsored by the Danforth Foundation. "Many educators agree that state tests serve no real purpose from a student's point of view, but students can use the tests to take a punch at what they see as the power structure."*

*The following is a conversation I had with a student that clearly shows the extent of this problem:*

**"Whatever."**

After reviewing the state test scores released over the summer, I noticed that Highflier Jones did not score at the minimum benchmark. This struck my attention because Highflier Jones took the ACT at the end of his junior year. He scored 30 on the first try. My adult logic could not make sense of this. If Highflier scored a 30 on the ACT, then he should have scored at least at the benchmark level on the state test.

As I looked closer at the scores of other students, I realized that many students scored much lower than I expected. Students inducted into the National Honor Society scored at much lower levels than their records suggested that they should. This aroused my curiosity. I knew Highflier personally. A little surly at times and some people felt that he was arrogant about his academic abilities, but I knew him as basically a nice kid. I decided that I would ask him to come by the office to talk.

Highflier arrived at the office around lunchtime, so I ordered a pizza from the local parlor and a couple of soft drinks for the two of us. After a few pleasantries and some catching up, we got to the real reason that I asked him to drop by.

*"We received the results on the state test and I was surprised at your score,"* I said. *"I thought that you would have scored higher."*

Highflier leaned back in his chair and studied my face as he prepared to reply.

A handsome young man, vice-president of the senior class in the upcoming school year, Highflier ran on the cross-country team and looked tall and lean in shorts and tee-shirt. His shortly cropped blond hair looked clean-cut. I wondered what went through his mind. I did not want to come across as confrontational or judgmental. I just wanted to quench my curiosity.

*"I was not real focused on the test,"* Highflier said as he looked away then back again. I said, *"These scores seem to go a little beyond a lack of focus. I know that you are smarter than these scores reflect."*

I inwardly grew angry with myself after my reply. I thought that perhaps my remark was too aggressive.
*"To be honest with you, I did not take the test seriously and I think that most kids don't,"* Highflier's body language tightened as he spoke.

*"Why don't students take the state tests seriously?* I asked. *"Don't they know that people in the community and in the state look at these scores and compare our school with other schools and make determinations about how good our school is based on those scores?"*

*"Why should students be interested in the state tests?"* Highflier explained. *"State tests really don't mean anything. They have no effect on college entrance. Employers do not use them to decide who gets the job. The military does not use them to decide if a person gets in or not, and they have no effect on grade point averages or credits at school. Actually from a student's point of view, they are completely worthless, a waste of time and energy."*

Highflier grew increasingly emotional as he talked. I realized that no matter how much I wanted students motivated to do well on the state tests, Highflier pointed out many truths. I felt compelled to defend the tests and I struggled for something that I could say that would make sense to a teenager.

*"You know of course that these tests could determine the value of your parent's real-estate property because when they sell their house there will be more of a demand if potential buyers feel that they are making a property purchase in a neighborhood inside of a top-notch school district,"* I weakly said.

Highflier paused for a moment as he looked at me and said, *"Yeah well, whatever."*

*Students embrace rebellion through passive resistance. The students strike by simply not taking the test seriously. They know that poor test scores cause educators to fear state or nationally invoked consequences, reputation loss, and unfair judgment of their professional abilities and dedication.* **To defend themselves, many educators openly criticize the accountability provisions of NCLB.** *Education Week magazine listed some of teachers' suggested alternatives:*

- *Replace "proficiency" with "grade level" expectations or another performance standard deemed more meaningful.*

- *Set more realistic goals for the amount of improvement schools must make from year to year.*
- *Permit states to use "growth" or "value-added" models, which track the progress of individual students over time. Design the growth targets so that all students reach the proficient level within a specified period.*
- *Expand the use of "accountability indexes" to include measures beyond test scores and give schools credit for students well above and below the proficient level.*
- *Identify schools for improvement, corrective action, or restructuring only if the same subgroup misses its performance targets in the same subject for two years in a row.*
- *Target the law's provision of choice and supplemental services to students in the subgroup that missed its performance targets—not the whole school population.*
- *Give more authority to states to design their own accountability systems as long as they make "significant" progress in the proportion of students at or above the proficient level and in closing achievement gaps.*
- *Move beyond test scores as the sole, or even the primary, measure for judging schools.*

*These alternatives, even if implemented, will not significantly improve test scores while students and their parents have no accountability. For example, American-black students and their parents often take tests less seriously than other demographic groups, leading to the most significant education question today: "Why do American-black students perform so poorly on standardized tests?"*

*Dialogue about achievement gaps in America prevails in intellectual conversations about education. Many gaps in achievement exist, such as the gap in math and science between genders, or the gap in achievement between low-resource people in a race and high-resource persons of the same race. Also, the gap on the high end between American-Asian students and American-white students concern many, but the gap on the low end mainly refers to the achievement gap between American-black and American-white students.*

### A Clear and Present Danger

*Education provides the adhesive that holds a democratic society together. Everyone who understands this must realize that the achievement gap threatens democracy and presents nothing less than a clear and present danger to American society and the ideas of economic free enterprise that fuels its prosperity. Politicians as prominent as the President of the United States, or as "grass roots" as local school board members openly acknowledge the achievement gap. This raised consciousness comes some years after the April 1983 National Commission on Excellence in Education "A Nation at Risk" report declared American education substandard.*

*The nation, in a sense, still reels from this report that became a catalyst to the Excellence in Education Movement, which gave birth to a plethora of school improvement initiatives. According to Richard Dufour and Robert Eaker in their book Professional Learning Communities, the Excellence in Education Movement failed because of a top-down approach, which gave way to the Restructuring Movement led by George Bush. In 1989, then President George H. Bush released his idea of a six-pointed national education set of goals and standards, "Goals 2000."*

1. *All children will start school ready to learn.*
2. *High school graduation rates will increase to at least 90 percent.*
3. *Students will leave grades four, eight, and twelve with competency in English, math, science, history and geography.*
4. *American students will rank first in the world in science and math.*
5. *Every American adult will be literate.*
6. *Every school will be drug-and-violence-free.*

*Congress later added two more goals:*

1. *Teachers will receive the professional development necessary to prepare students for the next century.*
2. *Schools will promote parental involvement and participation.*

*The components of "Goals 2000" were wonderful wants and desires that are easy to say. The question was, how can these goals be accomplished? What was the government going to do to facilitate the success of such high-minded thinking?*

*The sophistication with which Americans view the significance of education evolved over the years. As the country came under the leadership of George W. Bush, America took a different directive, "No Child Left Behind."*

*The NCLB decree is highly regarded by many Americans and speaks to the unacceptability of the low-end achievement gap. Many states across the nation followed this lead by initiating goals, performance, and knowledge standards that schools must require students to attain. Further, the educators in states that comply with NCLB construct tests that assess whether the students have the knowledge and can indeed perform at adequate levels.*

*These state-mandated tests illuminate the fact that American-black students score lower on standardized tests than do American-white students. But, more than the racial achievement gap, the results of these tests suggest that limited numbers of students of any color or race met the six points of "Goals 2000." Furthermore, if results of state tests prove valid, they suggest that the two movements spawned by "A Nation at Risk"— the Excellence in Education Movement and the Restructuring Movement—have had little or no positive academic effect on American students. Obviously something different must be done.*

***The complexity of the achievement gap affects the economic condition of American-black children.*** *According to the Goldberg Corporation, in St. Louis, Missouri, approximately 17 percent of the nation's American-black youngsters live in homes where the parents have incomes at or below the poverty line. The national poverty level was set at $18,104 for a family of four; $14,128 for a family of three; $11,569 for a married couple; and $9,039 for an individual. The schools that have the largest populations of American-black students also have the highest percentage of students receiving free and reduced lunch.*

*Those same school districts have the lowest taxes per student and the lowest assessed valuation. According to the commentary by Mary Futrell and Iris Rotberg, professors at George Washington University's school of education in the October 2, 2002 Education Week magazine, schools with predominately American-black students regularly receive the least amount of tax-based funding and private funding from parents, but have buildings most in need of repair and students that are most at-risk.*

**Simply put, the schools with the greater number of American-black students often have the most expenses with the least amount of money to spend.**

*Nevertheless, the students from these schools still have to compete against the students from schools with the most resources for acceptance into college and jobs and careers in the workplace.*

*Schools with large populations of American-black students and staff members usually receive the lowest scores on state audits for school improvement assessments and accountability initiatives. For instance, in the state of Missouri, schools with predominately American-black students and staffs receive a disproportionate number of deficient school and provisional accreditation labels.*

*Large percentages of American-black students score the lowest on state-created standardized tests. Furthermore, these schools receive low scores for such things as uncertified and non-subject expert teachers, when these same schools have difficulty attracting strong teachers because of low resources and high classroom challenges.*

### The Circle of Blame

*Furthermore, in this age of accountability, many people adopt the circular blame game to explain the achievement gap. The greater society blames the schools for the achievement gap because, after all, the schools are responsible for educating students. In this line of thinking, since American-black students do not achieve, the schools failed when they tried straightforward strategies to help American-black students do better on this or that test.*

*__Educators blame the parents__ for low scores on the state tests, accusing parents of failing in their roles as mentors and monitors of their children's achievement. The __parents blame society__ for the low scores on the state tests; no evidence exists that suggests abundant and clear rewards are available for students if they expend the time and energy necessary in the acquisition of success on state tests. The parents argue that limited proof supports the idea that success is available for American-black students who perform well on state tests. Hence, students invest less time and energy on something that probably will not bring comparable rewards. A portion of parents of American-black students realize a sad reality: unless American-blacks provide entertainment either as comedians, musicians, artists, or athletes, then few places in society exist for them beyond the most mundane jobs and vocations.*

*The newspapers, magazines and broadcast journalists constantly report that American society still blatantly discriminates against American-black people. According to the St. Louis Post Dispatch Newspaper October 3, 2002, American-black people who live in St. Louis have two to three times more chance to get turned down for mortgage loans than American-whites. Employers regularly hire last and fire first*

*American-blacks. American-blacks rarely hold high-level leadership positions within the economic structure of the country.*

*In the final analysis of the parents,* **society holds low expectations for American-black youngsters**, *who have limited genuine joy, adulation, reward, and satisfaction from the society when American-black people achieve outside of the world of entertainment. According to parents, lack of future employment prospects explains one reason why American-black students are less motivated to aspire toward achievement on standardized tests.*

### *Suggested Solutions to Motivate Students*

*In 2004, 51 percent of the schools in the state of Illinois failed to meet adequate yearly progress (AYP). Some states fared even worse. This data reveals that many American-white students also do not meet the benchmarks.* **Do students score low because they do not learn in school or because they do not give their best efforts on the tests?**

*To get closer to discovering this answer, we must find a way to motivate students to reach for success on the test. Individual schools could demonstrate a high regard for doing well on the state test by giving students a predetermined amount of credit toward graduation when students meet the test's benchmark. Students might receive a half credit for reaching the benchmark and a full credit if they score at the highest levels. Educators at individual schools could make these determinations collaboratively.*

**Business and government could cooperate in this effort by requiring students to have a work permit when they turn 16 years old in order to get a job.** *Students should then have to reach the minimum passing score on the state test in order to qualify for a work permit by age 16. Students that do not qualify by age 16 must then wait until they pass the test, reach age 19, or until high school graduation (whichever occurs first) to acquire a work permit.*

*Academically proficient teenage part-time workers could be quickly trained for jobs. The students would also better serve the companies for which they work. With teenage jobs usually hotly sought after,* **this plan creates a system where employers and school systems could work together**. *Further, teenagers who do not score at the minimum on the state tests really do not have time for part-time employment; extra study time might be a better use of their time.*

*In all of my years in education administration, in two states, at eight schools, in seven school districts, I have noticed that students make higher grades with fewer behavior problems in driver education than in any other class in school and every student wants to take the class.* **To qualify to take the driver education class, students should be required to meet the minimum on the state test** *when given in the middle school years. Also, students should reach at least the minimum level on the state test during the high school years in order to qualify for a driver's license.*

*Students who do not qualify by age 16 must then wait until they pass the test, reach age 19, or until high school graduation (whichever occurs first) to acquire a driving permit. This restriction would put more responsible youngsters behind the wheel of a car. Automobile insurance companies discovered that students with high academics have fewer accidents.* **This restriction might also save the lives of hundreds of teenagers since automobile accidents are the main cause of deaths among teenagers.**

*Most colleges and universities now give placement tests to entering freshmen. When students do not pass these tests they must take remediation courses in math or communication arts. These courses cost hundreds of dollars and do not count toward the requirements for graduation.*

**Colleges and universities could help motivate high school students toward achievement on state tests if they waive placement testing and obligations to take remediation classes to those students that reach the benchmark on the test in their state.**

**Tuition could be waved for the first year for students that score in the highest categories on the state test.**
*These motivational initiatives would certainly raise the awareness of parents and students concerning the state tests and would create incentives for students to do well on the assessments. Students would focus on lessons during school, especially in schools that employ the Systemic Learning Cycle. Student perception concerning the importance of academic lessons would increase.*

*These initiatives might also motivate students toward graduation and away from dropping out. If a student does not meet qualification for a work permit or driving license through state testing, then graduation becomes an intelligent "plan B." If a student does not reach qualification through state testing then does not graduate, they penalize themselves by having to wait until age 19 to acquire work permits and a driving license.*

*Another way to motivate students to have a greater sense of urgency when they take a state test would be to encourage parental attention and involvement.* **The federal government could make a huge impact on such a concept by allowing a significant income tax deduction for each student that reaches the benchmark on the state standardized test** *when the family files their income tax with the IRS. Families could get a significant deduction for every child they have that reaches exceed levels on state tests. The scale for deductions could slide to reflect income; those with lower incomes would get a larger deduction and as incomes elevate deduction amounts would decrease. This incentive might cause low-income parents to generate more of a sense of concern about their child's academic development and become increasingly interested in what is occurring academically in the schools where their youngsters attend.*

### Immediate Threat
*The problem of low achievement immediately threatens a capitalistic democracy. This must be confronted with determined assertiveness. Students must realize that getting smart takes hard work and the hard work that leads to getting smart brings gratification deferred, but nevertheless positive. Entities within society should recognize and embrace students who display high achievement on test scores. Students that score well on state tests should receive affirmation, attention, praise and opportunity from the adults within the institutions and society.*

*Entities within society can collaborate to make a real difference in the academic development of students by having high expectations, rewarding achievement, and compensating effective effort from the students. Business people, professionals, parents, and politicians demand rightly that schools have high expectations for all of the children. But* **business people, the media, professionals, parents, politicians, and every microcosm of society must make certain that quality earns rewards so that children have easily recognizable evidence that academic success brings achievement at all levels regardless of race, gender, religion, or preceding economic condition.** *The real answer to student achievement problems comes when people in society stop pointing fingers and everyone works together to find solutions.*

- ***Parents*** *must admit that education offers the safest way for their children to gain economic prosperity, a lucrative, worthwhile career, and learn the nuances of mainstream American society.*

- ***The corporate community*** *must admit that institutions of education offer the best place to find large numbers of qualified workers. Institutions of education offer the best place to find a large selection of workers with strong leadership skills. Institutions of education offer the best place to find workers with creativity and higher level critical thinking skills.*

- ***Students*** *must realize that for an overwhelming majority of them, education offers the most consistent road to success in life.*

*Sincerely,*
*Dr. Edward Harris*
*Principal*

# Epilogue

## Developing a Lesson Design Model

The QUO Process explains how teachers can work together on teacher teams to develop a circular construct where there is a certain method for constructing lesson units. Using this philosophy, the lesson process does not end with the unit test; the analysis component of the process begins where the test ends. Teachers would discover students that need extra help and students that are high achievers and provide recovery and enrichment techniques to help the students in their further development. Teachers should analyze their delivery strategies and methods and make appropriate changes for future lessons on the topic.

Develop and Present Authentic Lessons Use Common Assessments

Review and Analyze Data To Identify Struggling Students

Create a Collection of Recovery and Enrichment Activities

Traditionally, teachers, once hired, are assigned a room and the teacher then is left to teach classes on his or her own. This practice actually isolates teachers and cuts them off from each other. Over years teachers have drifted further apart and rarely share information with each other. The "whole village" concept is not occurring inside schools. In many schools teachers are not helping each other teach as much as they could.

To accelerate and intensify student learning, teachers could implement operational collectives, collaborative cooperatives, dyad teaching teams, and core curriculum teaching teams to implement the QUO Process and help the transition to Collaborative School Transformation. Each collective of teachers would collaborate to decide how each team would individually and uniquely address each area of QUO Process. Each collective would design a procedure for creating order, unity, and quality that they would adhere to as a team.

The collectives would individually establish how each would create order among the students that are assigned to each teacher in each collective. Each collective of teachers would determine how to interact with parents of their students to protect the learning environment by implementing parallel supervision. Each collective would create a discipline system to employ when the students assigned to the teachers within the collective behave inappropriately. The discipline systems would be based on de-escalation and creating a learning experience designed to help students gain strategies that will improve behavior.

Teachers within each collective would design a structure that embraces unity by agreeing upon a systemic learning cycle. Within this cycle the teachers would review the course offerings in their department to discover if there need to be additions or deletions, authenticate the curriculum to make certain that information that will appear on the state test is covered at some point in the course, and state descriptors are observed in lesson units. Teachers in each collective would entertain ideas surrounding assessment-based instruction by creating quarterly common assessments and developing systematic lesson delivery models.

To ensure the quality of student learning, teachers within each collective would discover ways to manage direct data. Each collective of teachers would collect data based on the quarterly common assessments, and other performance event assignments. Struggling students would be identified and advanced students would be identified as well. Correctives would be designed for struggling students while enrichments would be designed for those that are advanced.

The implementation of teacher teams would break the status quo by bringing small groups of teachers together to plan and work together to be better prepared to engage student learning. Teachers within collectives could become guest speakers in the classes of partner teachers within the collective. Teachers from different collectives could cooperate and become guest speakers forming cross curriculum partnerships.

## How to Measure the Results From Implementing QUO

Once QUO Process is in place, to discover its effectiveness several indicators can be cited to determine success. Three subjective indicators can be used; it can be asked, "Has the culture and climate, general civility, and student decorum improved?" Objective indicators may be divided into five components; improved behavior, attendance, grades, standardized test scores, and athletic success.

- **Improved behavior** in the school can be determined by fewer detentions, fewer out of school suspensions, fewer expulsions, fewer in-school suspensions, fewer fights, fewer assaults, fewer weapons, and fewer thefts.
- **Improved attendance** in the school can be determined by higher percentage of teacher and student attendance, and decline in tardiness.
- **Improved student grades** can be determined by fewer failing grades earned by students, and more straight A and honor role students.

- **Improved standardized test scores** can be determined by the increased number of students that meet the benchmark, the increased number of students that reach the exceed category, and the reduced number of students that fall in the low category.
- **Improved athletic success** can be observed by more games and conference team championships being won, more conference honors for individual students being awarded, and teams regularly advancing in state competitions.

## EMBED THE QUO PROCESS BY TAKING IT A STEP FURTHER

To truly embed the QUO Process within a school district, educators would need the courage to fully embrace a program of total Collaborative School Transformation. The QUO Process embraces the ideas inherent within green culture and is a component of **Collaborative School Transformation**—enhanced by **EnTeam concepts**. Quo Process can help educators develop a **"blue print"** for working together to initiate the implementation of strategies in schools that will raise the academic performance of students.

**Collaborative School Transformation (CST)** fosters quality, unity, and order in education by learning to win together. With CST, a new "schoolhouse" can be built where a framework for promoting academic achievement among all students exist. Implementation of CST gives a plan and brings direction to a school which will lead to a better school climate, higher staff and morale, improved trust within the community, and increased critical thinking skills and learning among students.

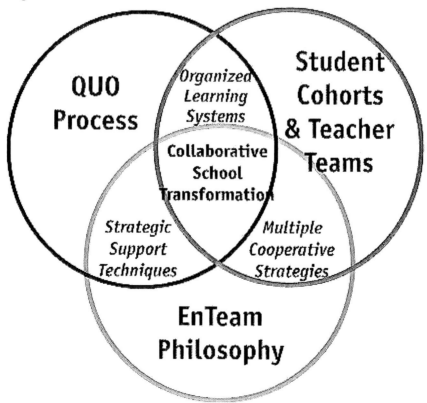

Although the QUO Process has been thoroughly explained the other two components of Collaborative School Transformation (CST) are equally important:

1. **The EnTeam Philosophy:** Developed by Ted Wohlfarth, EnTeam strives to increase productivity and cooperation in schools by providing activities that challenge students, teachers, and parents to win together. The unique benefit of EnTeam activities is that they provide specific ways to actually **measure cooperation.** Strategies are developed so that participants can keep score based on collaborative problem solving. When combined, QUO Process and the EnTeam concept of winning together create Collaborative School Transformation. Ted Wohlfarth, developer of EnTeam, directs the EnTeam activities and explains the EnTeam concept in his book Learning to Win Together. When combined with strategies of the QUO Process, EnTeam activities encourage the development of strategic support techniques. Such support techniques can be used to bring those within the Learning Triad together and strongly advocate teamwork where one component will not be satisfied until those in the other two components are successful. The implementation of multiple cooperation strategies is central to the success of Collaborative School Transformation.

2. **Teacher teams and Student Cohorts:** To best accomplish Collaborative School Transformation there must be a framework for the organization of the people where relationships between those in the Learning Triad can be more effectively developed over time. This framework merges with the QUO Process to create and support organized learning systems to nurture the academic achievement of students. To gain trust and teamwork within the Learning Triad, parents would commit to Parallel Supervision, students would be determined to give effective effort in their classes, and educators would immerse themselves in the QUO Process as Collaborative School Transformation engulfs a school district.

**My next book will cover Shepherding Teams in more detail.**

# Appendix

## Table 1

## EnTeam Survey
Learning to Win Together®

**Please let us know your opinion about school:**

**A. Do you agree or disagree with each of the following statements about this school?**

*Circle one number for each statement:*

|  | Strongly Agree | Tend to Agree | Tend to Disagree | Strongly Disagree |
|---|---|---|---|---|
| 1. I am pleased with the education that my child receives at this school. | 1 | 2 | 3 | 4 |
| 2. The teachers help my child to be excited about learning. | 1 | 2 | 3 | 4 |

| | | | |
|---|---|---|---|
| 3. I receive clear information about how well my child is doing at school. | 1 | 2 | 3 | 4 |
| 4. I have information about the school's overall plan to uplift all students' grades and behavior. | 1 | 2 | 3 | 4 |
| 5. The school gives me the information I need to help my child do well in school. | 1 | 2 | 3 | 4 |
| 6. I feel welcome to visit school and talk with people in the office. | 1 | 2 | 3 | 4 |
| 7. When I call or visit the school, I receive prompt and courteous service. | 1 | 2 | 3 | 4 |
| 8. I feel welcome to visit with the principal and ask questions. | 1 | 2 | 3 | 4 |
| 9. I feel welcome to talk with my child's teachers and ask questions. | 1 | 2 | 3 | 4 |

10. When I leave a message at school, the people at school return my call promptly.

    1        2        3        4

11. When my child is struggling or needs help, the teachers let me know how I can help.

    1        2        3        4

12. I have met parents of other students at my child's school.

    1        2        3        4

13. I have been invited to help with projects at school.

    1        2        3        4

14. I have been invited to be a member of the parent organization at school.

    1        2        3        4

15. My opinion counts at school.

    1        2        3        4

**B. What do you think would help your child(ren) be more successful at this school?** *Write in your answer*

**Please turn in this survey as soon as possible. Thank you!**

174

## TABLE 2
## RESULTS-ORIENTED TEACHER ASSESSMENT

| **Standard 1: Protecting the Learning Environment (Improved communication and implementation of parallel supervision)** |
| --- |

*The teacher demonstrates commitment to improving communication and implements parallel supervision.*

Score as follows: A=4, B=3, C=3, D=1, F=0, G=0 (question not counted)

_____1. The teacher has evidence that he or she is inviting and reaching out to parents and students by:

        A.    Doing two or more of the below at least once a semester
        B.    Serving on district committees with parents and colleagues
        C.    Coaching or sponsoring extra-curricula activities
        D.    Serving on a building committee
        F.    Does not participate in any of the above
        G.    Not observed

_____2. The teacher demonstrates commitment to improving communication by:

        A.    Doing two or more of the below
        B.    Calling 10 or more homes of students weekly
        C.    Coaching or sponsoring extra-curricula activities
        D.    Attending parent-teacher conferences
        F.    Not obvious
        G.    Not observed

_____3. The teacher attends or helps supervise extracurricular activities:

        A.    Home and away events each week
        B.    Home events once or twice a month
        C.    Events once a months
        D.    One or two events each semester
        F.    Less than one event per semester
        G.    Not observed

_____4. The teacher provides information to families about the instructional program.

     A.    Four times a year

     B.    Three times a year

     C.    Twice a year

     D.    Once a year

     F.    Less than once a year

     G.    Not observed

_____5. The teacher makes phone calls to 10 or more families per week to provide academic information about students:

     A.    Every week of the month

     B.    Three weeks in a month

     C.    Two weeks in a month

     D.    One week in a month

     F.    Less than one week each month

     G.    Not observed

_____6. The teacher has evidence that he or she has communicated the classroom boundaries and academic expectations to those in the Learning Triad:

     A.    Has record of communicating this to parents, students, and administration

     B.    Has record of communicating this to parents only

     C.    Has record of communicating this to students only

     D.    Has record of communicating this to administration only

     F.    Has no record of communicating this to anyone

     G.    Not observed

_____7. The teacher has evidence that he or she has developed systems of support and monitoring for students:

     A.    The teacher has written explanations of support opportunities and monitoring strategies that have been communicated to parents, students, and administrators

     B.    The teacher has written explanations of support opportunities and monitoring strategies that have been communicated to parents

     C.    The teacher has written explanations of support opportunities and monitoring strategies that have been communicated to students

     D.    The teacher has written explanations of support opportunities and monitoring strategies that have been communicated with administrators

     F.    The teacher has written explanations of support opportunities **or** monitoring strategies, but not both

     G.    Not observed

_____8. The teacher has evidence that he or she has developed a consequence scale:

A. The teacher has the consequences for inappropriate behavior in class posted and has sent the explanation to parents, students, and teacher team members

B. The teacher has the consequences for inappropriate behavior in class posted and has sent the explanation to parents

C. The teacher has the consequences for inappropriate behavior in class posted and has presented written information to students

D. The teacher has the consequences for inappropriate behavior in class posted and has presented written information to teacher team members

F. The teacher does not have the consequences for inappropriate behavior in class posted and has not distributed the explanation to members of the Learning Triad

G. Not observed

_____9. The teacher has evidence that there is a strategy in place to praise, recognize, and grant privileges to students that comply with school behavioral boundaries and academic expectations:

A. The teacher has a record of strategies for praise, .recognition, rewards, and privileges

B. The teacher has a record of strategies for three of the four

C. The teacher has a record of strategies for two of the four

D. The teacher has a record of strategies for one of the four

F. The teacher has no record of strategies for praise, recognition, rewards, or privileges

G. Not observed

_____10. The teacher follows the policies and procedures of the school district:

A. Always

B. Most of the time

C. Some of the time

D. Once or twice

F. Never

G. Not observed

# Standard 2: Apply Effective Pedagogy (Authenticated Curriculum and Assessment-Based Instruction)

*The teacher demonstrates that he or she plans lessons within the framework of the Systemic Learning Cycle.*

_____11. The teacher has evidence that he or she uses the systemic learning cycle when developing learning units:

- A.   For all lesson units
- B.   In five of every six lesson units
- C.   In four of every six lesson units
- D.   In three of every six lesson units
- F.   In two of every six lesson units
- G.   Not observed

_____12. The teacher has evidence that he or she uses authenticated curriculum and the lessons are tied to the state frameworks and descriptors:

- A.   Each time
- B.   Most of the time
- C.   Some of the time
- D.   Seldom
- F.   Never
- G.   Not observed

_____13. The teacher has evidence that he or she uses assessment-based instruction strategies when designing lessons:

- A.   To all lesson units
- B.   In five of every six lesson units
- C.   In four of every six lesson units
- D.   In three of every six lesson units
- F.   In two of every six lesson units
- G.   Not observed

_____14. The teacher collaborates with colleagues to develop common assessments:

- A.   For all lesson units
- B.   In five of every six lesson units
- C.   In four of every six lesson units
- D.   In three of every six lesson units
- F.   In two of every six lesson units
- G.   Not observed

_____15. The teacher uses common assessments:

      A.    All four quarters

      B.    Three of four quarters

      C.    Two of four quarters

      D.    One of four quarters

      F.    Does not use common assessments

      G.    Not observed

_____16. The teacher uses the learning styles delivery model when presenting lessons:

      A.    All four components were observed

      B.    Three of the four components were observed

      C.    Two of the four components were observed

      D.    One of the four components were observed

      F.    None of the four components were observed

      G.    Not observed

_____17. The teacher uses technology and a variety of resources to enhance student learning at least:

      A.    Four times a month

      B.    Three times a month

      C.    Two times a month

      D.    Once a month

      F.    Less than once a month

      G.    Not observed

_____18. The teacher uses a variety of learning styles when presenting lessons:

      A.    All four learning styles were observed

      B.    Three of the four learning styles were observed

      C.    Two of the four learning styles were observed

      D.    One of the four learning styles was observed

      F.    None of the four learning styles were observed

      G.    Not observed

_____19. The teacher asks questions to stimulate higher order thinking:

      A.    Four or more higher-order questions were asked

      B.    Three higher order questions were asked

      C.    Two higher order questions were asked

      D.    One higher order question was asked

      F.    No higher order questions were asked

      G.    Did not observe

_____20. The lessons observed are tied to the school improvement plan:

    A.    Tightly tied

    B.    Loosely tied

    C.    Slightly tied

    D.    Referenced

    F.    Not mentioned

    G.    Not observed

# Standard 3: Manage Direct Data (Identifying struggling students and high achieving students)

*The teacher has evidence that he or she uses direct data to identify struggling students and revise lessons.*

_____21. The teacher has evidence that the unit tests given correspond to the standardized test form.

    A.    For all tests taken

    B.    For 75 percent of the tests taken

    C.    For 50 percent of the tests taken

    D.    For only one of the tests taken

    F.    For none of the tests taken

    G.    Not observed

_____22. The teacher has evidence that he or she collects data from tests, performance events, and constructed response activities:

    A.    For all activities assessed

    B.    For three fourths of the activities assessed

    C.    For one half of the activities assessed

    D.    For only one of the activities assessed

    F.    For none of the activities assessed

    G.    Not observed

_____23. The teacher has evidence that he or she uses the information from the collected data to identify students who need recovery strategies:

    A.    For all tests taken

    B.    For three fourths of the tests taken

    C.    For half of the tests taken

    D.    For only one of the tests taken

    F.    For none of the tests taken

    G.    Not observed

_____24. The teacher has evidence that he or she uses the information from the collected data to identify students who should be offered enrichment activities.

      A.    For all tests taken

      B.    For three fourths of the tests taken

      C.    For half of the tests taken

      D.    For only one of the tests taken

      F.    For none of the tests taken

      G.    Not observed

_____25. The teacher has evidence that he or she uses the information from the collected data to self-evaluate, identify struggling and achieving students, and to revise plans and tests:

      A.    For all four

      B.    For three of the four

      C.    For two of the four

      D.    For one of the four

      F.    None of the four

      G.    Not observed

_____26. The students in the teacher's classes achieve at acceptable levels on the common assessments:

      A.    80 percent or more of the students passed the common assessments

      B.    70 to 79.9 percent of the students passed the common assessments

      C.    50 to 69.9 percent of the students passed the common assessments

      D.    40 to 49.9 percent of the students passed the common assessments

      F.    Less than 40 percent of the students passed the common ssessments

      G.    40 percent or more of the students tested had IEP's

# Standard 4:  Creating Interventions for Academic Support

*The teacher has evidence that he or she uses interventions to assist identified struggling students.*

_____27. The teacher uses the school-wide academic intervention initiatives to assist students during lesson delivery units:

      A.    For all delivery units

      B.    For three fourths of the delivery units

      C.    For one half of the delivery units

D.    For only one of the delivery units

F.    For none of the delivery units

G.    Not observed

_____28.  The teacher has evidence that he or she uses self-made academic intervention initiatives to assist students:

A.    For all delivery units

B.    For three fourths of the delivery units

C.    For half of the delivery units

D.    For only one of the delivery units

F.    For none of the delivery units

G.    Not observed

_____29.  The teacher has evidence that he or she uses math and reading software to assist students during:

A.    All delivery units

B.    Three fourths of the delivery units

C.    Half of the delivery units

D.    Only one of the delivery units

F.    None of the delivery units

G.    Not observed

_____30.  The teacher has evidence that he or she uses state and national test software to help prepare students for taking standardized tests:

A.    Each week

B.    Each month

C.    Each quarter

D.    Each semester

F.    Never

G.    Not observed

_____31.  The teacher has evidence that he or she uses Internet access to help prepare students for taking standardized tests:

A.    At least once a week

B.    At least once a month

C.    At least once a quarter

D.    At least once a semester

F.    Less than once a semester

G.    Not observed

## Scoring Rubric

**A= 4 points**
**B= 3 points**
**C= 2 points**
**D= 1 point**
**F= 0 points**
G= Disregard question
**(Total points then divide by number of questions to get an average)**

# Ratings to Determine Compensation

- *Teachers receiving a rating of 3.45 to 4. would receive 100 percent of the school board-approved pay increase.*
- *Teachers receiving a rating of 2.95 to 3.44 would receive 75 percent of the school board-approved pay increase.*
- *Teachers receiving a rating of 2.45 to 2.94 would receive 50 percent of the school board-approved pay increase.*
- *Teachers receiving a rating of 1.95 and 2.44 would receive 20 percent of the school board-approved pay increase. If a teacher in this category fails to move him or herself to proficiency (2.45 or above) within the year, then he or she would receive a "Failure to Reach Proficiency" notice. If he or she fails to reach proficiency one year after the notice, then the district would terminate him or her.*

*Teachers receiving a rating of 1.94 or below would receive no pay increase and would immediately receive a "Failure to Reach Proficiency" notice. If tenured, the district would grant one year to move performance to proficiency. If a teacher in this category failed to comply, then the district would terminate him or her. The district would terminate an untenured teacher in this category at the end of the school year.*

# Glossary of Terms Common to Education

**ABSTRACT THINKING** – The ability to converse about concepts that are not empirical

**AESTHETICS** – Attention to beauty, décor, pleasantness

**AFFIRMATION** – A follow-up comment concerning a student response that embellishes or substantiates the remark

**ALIGNMENT, EXTERNAL** – The measurable learner objectives and related activities and assessments reflect state knowledge standards at the appropriate learning level

**ALIGNMENT, INTERNAL** – There is clear correlation among measurable learner objectives, instructional activities, and assessments

**ANALYTICAL LEARNERS** – Those students who prefer thinking in abstract, working alone, manipulating objects to enhance learning and interacting with the teacher

**ARTICULATION** – How the curriculum fits together among grade levels and courses within a subject; an exercise to ensure that essential skills and knowledge are introduced, practiced, mastered, and reviewed at the appropriate grade/developmental level

**ARTICULATION AGREEMENT** – Written agreements between school districts and postsecondary institutions to ensure that students completing vocational programs can continue their education after high school

**AUTHENTIC ASSESSMENT** – Test demanding the application of skills and knowledge in a "real-life" situation

**BENCHMARK** – Expected or anticipated skill or understanding at various developmental levels; a specified step along a path toward achievement of a goal or standard

**CAROUSELING** – Groups move to a variety of stations completing tasks then moving on

**CLOSURE** – An organized ending to a lesson

**COMPREHENSION CHECK** – Using ways to determine if students have a working understanding of information

**COMPREHENSIVE SCHOOL IMPROVEMENT PLAN (CSIP)** – Long-range plan developed by the district with involvement by staff, board, parents, patrons to address needs of the district

**CONCEPTUAL LEARNING** – Understanding a whole idea – not just parts

**COOPERATIVE GROUPS** – Dividing students into teams where each has a definite role, a previously defined goal or project to complete

**COOPERATIVE LEARNING** – Students work in organized groups to learn; roles are assigned to each member of the group and each is accountable for mastery of the concept being learned

185

**CORRECTIVES** – When the teacher implements ways to help students who are experiencing difficulty with the current project

**CONSTRUCTED RESPONSE ITEMS** – These items ask a student to give their own short answer rather than choosing from a list of possible answers

**COURSE OBJECTIVE** – Broad expectation for a course of study or individual course

**CROSS-REFERENCE** – Objectives are matched, either in part or whole, with some aspects of the Show-Me-Standards; without specific focus, may or may not represent a match

**CURRICULUM** – The plan for the presentation of educational activities in an educational institution

**CURRICULUM FRAMEWORKS** – State frameworks for curriculum development-intended to guide schools as they develop local curriculum aligned to the state standards

**DELVING** – Questioning in such a way as to pull additional information from a student by compelling more thought

**DESISTING** – Intervening when student behavior is inappropriate

**DISAGGREGATED DATA** – Data that is separated in order to study the performance of various groups within a total population

**EMPATHIZING** – Having genuine feelings and concern for someone else's situation

**ENTEAM** – The process of bringing people together to solve problems collaboratively and measuring their performance as cooperators; organizing people into win-win relationships

**EQUITABLE DISTRIBUTION** – Involving students, from all parts of the room, in the lesson

**EQUITY** – Equal treatment, equal rights, equal access for all populations, and/or multi-cultural perspectives and cultural diversity concepts

**ESTABLISHING SET** – Creating an atmosphere that will lead students to become interested in the upcoming lesson by the use of activities or discussions, which personalize lesson

**EXTRAPOLATING** – Extending a concept to relate to an idea or entity otherwise unconnected to the original thought

**FLEXIBLE GROUPING** – Temporary groups formed on the basis of assessment results to receive instruction in specific reading strategies and skills, usually with text at the students' instructional level

**GRADUATE GOALS** – A description of how a subject/course supports the district's goals for graduates; in the absence of graduate goals, objectives cross-referenced to state standards in a board-adopted guide will imply adoption of the standards as the graduate goals

**GUIDED PRACTICE** – Teacher helps students along while they practice some task

**HYPOTHESIZING** – An untested assumption

**IMAGING** – Individuals visualize a situation or concept for a quiet time

**INDEPENDENT PRACTICE** – Students practice an explained task on their own

**INNOVATING** – Fresh, new, and different thinking about an issue

**INSPIRATIONAL DIALOGUE** – Encouraging students to try to take a risk; teacher expresses belief that they will succeed

**INTERPRETING** – Making an occurrence or intellectual response more understandable

**INTUITIVE FEELING (IF)**– Students like concept formation, metaphorical problem solving, creative problem solving, write to learn, independent study, and simulation

**JIGSAW** – Members of groups become expert at information then move to form different groups where they teach others

**KINDLING ACTIVITY** – A four-step process for students: 1. Visualize a task, concept, or reaction. 2. Think about it briefly. 3. Write responses. 4. Share with neighbor, discuss differences

**LATENCY** – "Wait time" after a question is asked. Allowing students an opportunity to collect thoughts before an answer

**LEARNING ENHANCERS** – Objects or materials placed around the room, which demonstrate or relate information in an interesting way

**LECTURING** – The teacher talks to the students from a prepared text or memory

**LINKING** – Making a connection between seemingly unconnected thoughts

**LOGICAL SEQUENCING** – Have the lesson follow in successive steps, one step leading to the next

**MASTERY LEARNING** – Student's ability to remember and repeat facts and skills

**METAPHORIC EXPLANATION** – Create an analogy, use an explanation of one thing to show that it is like something else

**MODELING IDEAL BEHAVIOR** – Displaying desired behavior so that students can see how it looks

**MUSIC IN CLASSROOM** – Recorded music of a variety, short informative explanations, or simply playing music softly in the background

**OPENING VIGNETTE** – Telling a short story that holds some type of analogy to the general lesson

**OUTCOME** – Expected or anticipated result of an instructional activity for a learner

**PAIRS** – Two individuals work together toward a predetermined end

**PEER COACHING** – Learning or improving knowledge or skills with the help of staff or students of equal standing

**PEER TEACHING** – When one student teaches another student

**PERFORMANCE EVENT** – Complex demonstration of student knowledge (i.e., project, speech, essay, concept map, experiments, research paper, etc)

**"PIGGYBACK"** – To expand or add on to a comment previously made by someone

**POSTULATE** – Make an educated prediction from a learned body of knowledge

**PRACTICE BY DOING** – Students are given the opportunity to practice a technique recently taught to them by the teacher

**PROVIDING INPUT** – Sharing information about a topic or providing helpful information to students in need

**PROXIMITY** – Moving about the room and getting close to students

**RATIONALE** – A reason or justification for teaching the subject/course related to the district's mission and philosophy that is printed in the curriculum guide

**RELATIONAL LEARNERS** – Those students who prefer talking while they think, working in pairs or groups, interacting with others to enhance learning and conversing with those around them

**REORGANIZE INFORMATION** – Rephrasing or restructuring the shared information

**RESPONSIVENESS** – Reacting to student interrogatives or non-verbal cues

**RUBRIC** – Scoring guide with written expectations or levels necessary to earn a certain point value or grade

**SCOPE AND SEQUENCE OUTLINE** – Concrete, often graphic or tabular representation of the presentation of the learner objectives. Scope is the latitude or breadth of the curriculum and sequence is the time order and/or grade level of the presentation of educational experiences

**SELF-STUDY** – The school district's responses to all of the state standards and indicators

**SENSING FEELING (SF)** – Students like graduated difficulty, team games, tournaments, jigsaw, collaborative problem solving, role-playing

**SENSING THINKING (ST)** – Students like lecture, practice, programmed instruction, gradual difficulty, mastery

**SHOW & TELL** – Groups prepare one member to move out and share group-initiated ideas with other groups

**STANDARD** – Expected level of quality or excellence against which judgments and accreditation decisions are made

**STATING FOCUS** – Revealing the direction of the lesson either verbally or by a list of objectives

**STRATEGIC PLANNING** – Formal long-range planning effort that involves school staff, district patrons and others. Elements include developing and refining a plan as well as the steps necessary to implement the components of the plan upon board approval

**STUDENT TALK** – Student to student discussion about class work

**TEACHER CREATED MODEL –** A specific way to accomplish a task is outlined by the teacher

**TERSE** – Short, and to the point

**VISUAL ORGANIZER** – Sorting brain-stormed or other information so that the organization can be easily seen

# References

1. Barnes, Julian E. "Unequal Education, Now the Focus Shifts from Integration to Achievement for all," U.S. News & World Report, pages 68-69, March 22-29 2004
2. Brown, Cynthia Stokes (2001) <u>Refusing Racism, White Allies and the Struggle for Civil Rights</u>
3. Catsambis, S. (2001) "Expanding knowledge of parental involvement in children's secondary education: Connections with high school senior's academic success." Social Psychology of Education, 5, 149-177
4. Clark, Ron (2003) <u>The Essential 55</u>
5. Cooper, Eric (2004) <u>Teaching All The Children</u>, (Chapter 2)
6. Dufore, Rick (2001) <u>Professional Learning Communities</u>
7. Epstein, J. L. (2001). "School, family, and community partnerships: Preparing educators and improving schools." Educational Leadership May 2004  Volume 61 Number 8
8. Howard, Gary, (2002) <u>We Can't Teach What We Don't Know</u>
9. Jenkins, William, (2004) <u>Understanding and Educating African-American Children</u>
10. Ladson-Billings, Gloria (1999) <u>The Dreamkeepers: Successful Teachers of African-American Children</u>
11. National Association of Secondary School Principals, (2004) <u>Breaking Ranks II: Strategies for Leading High School Reform</u>
12. Sergiovanni, Thomas (2004) <u>Leadership for the Schoolhouse</u>
13. Smith, Rosa A. "Saving Black Boys: The Elusive Promise of Public Education", The American Prospect, February 2004, no. 2, vol. 15, pp49-50., The American Prospect, Inc., Boston, MA.
14. St. John, Edward and Louis Miron, (2002) <u>Reinterpreting Urban School Reform</u>
15. Thernstrom, Abigail and Stephan, (2002) <u>No Excuses</u>
16. Wohlfarth, Theodore A., (2005), <u>Win Together in Education</u>

## ABOUT THE AUTHOR:

### *Dr. Edward Harris, Principal, Cahokia High School in Cahokia, Illinois, and Developer of the QUO Process*

Dr. Harris has worked in education for over 27 years and has won numerous awards, including the Good Apple Award and in 1999 the Illinois State Principal of the Year award. After graduate study at the University of Illinois Dr. Harris later earned a Ph.D. in education curriculum at the University of Berkley, Michigan, a Specialist Degree in Administration and Superintendency at Truman University in Kirksville Missouri, a Masters of Education at Maryville University in St. Louis, and a Bachelor of Science degree in Social Studies for Secondary Education at the University of Missouri-St. Louis. He taught for 10 years in the Parkway School District in St. Louis MO. He has also coached football and women's basketball for more than 15 years at both the high school and college levels. Dr. Harris has served as adjunct professor at both Maryville and Southern Illinois at Edwardsville Universities.

Prior to serving as principal at Cahokia, Dr. Harris was the principal at Quincy, Edwardsville, IL, and at Oakville High School in a suburb of St. Louis, Missouri. Dr. Harris has served as an administrator in a variety of locations; he served as Assistant Superintendent in the Normandy School District, and began his administrative career as assistant principal in the Parkway and Ladue School Districts in St. Louis, Missouri. His wide experience base includes work in rural, urban, and suburban schools. Dr. Harris has written several articles and in the year 2000 published a book about parenting teenagers entitled *A Letter from the Principal.* He can be reached at: ejh@enteam.org

Printed in the United States
48275LVS00002BB/145-240

9 781420 884340